4-42220
β 15°
Georgian
Locomotive

The   Georgian   Locomotive

The Fabric of Steam.

The Georgian Locomotive

Some elegant steam locomotive power in
the South and Southwest, 1918-1945,
an episode in American taste

by *H. Stafford Bryant, Jr.*

WEATHERVANE BOOKS
NEW YORK

In fond memory of Morris Blake Mount, devotee of the steam loco-motives of the Southern Railway

Contents

List of Illustrations

Foreword

THIS BOOK explores a neglected side of railroad history. Volumes have been devoted to the locomotive. A few have dwelt on its architecture incidentally; none, to my knowledge, primarily. Yet there has always been an esthetic side to locomotive design. When in 1838, I. K. Brunel ordered engines for the Great Western, he insisted that they not only be big and fast, but as handsome as could be made — because, as he put it, "a plain young lady, however amiable, is apt to be neglected."

In Victorian locomotives, beauty and performance were meant to complement each other. Gothic cabs, Grecian domes and gingerbread detail lent taste to early American machinery. For British engineers, nothing less than an architecture of locomotion would do. Shunning the expedient, they built according to a formal ideal, a discipline of reason and order. Classical principles — simplicity, symmetry and clarity — shaped the structure of locomotion from chaste, cabless engine profiles, to the effortless, perpetual motion of huge, centered single drivers neatly flanked by leading and trailing axles, right down to an absolutely straight and level track. Progress and practical reality would eventually demolish the symmetry of the structure, but the discipline of simplicity and clarity spurred a design tradition that became the classic standard of locomotive style.

It is the revival of classic style on American railroads in the years between the first and second World Wars, and the last grand flourish of the American steam locomotive, of which Stu Bryant writes. Standardization and efficiency had stripped away the once distinctive Victorian embellishments, complexes of pipes and rods replaced the picturesque gingerbread. The extraordinary pile of twentieth century locomotive hardware to be packed within clearances set by Victorian wood burners seemed to leave no room for esthetics. Yet the last decades of steam produced some of the handsomest engines ever to appear on American rails. In classic locomotive style, the structure itself is the form. The pleasure of sheer line, shape and proportion of mechanical structure, articulated rather than embellished by color, lining and lettering, transformed what might have been lumbering centipedes into the grand, even graceful architecture the author here recalls.

Today this architecture has all but disappeared from the American scene. To another generation, the exciting combination of massive geometry and mechanical action of classic locomotives will be a forgotten experience. Few will know the impact it had on those who lived in the Age of Steam. Writers from Victor Hugo to Thomas Wolfe seized upon the sight and sound of speeding locomotives to convey the visual and emotional realities of modern life. For the pioneers of modern design, dissatisfied with Victorian gentility and eclectic facades, the locomotive became the symbol of machine-age design, a starting point for a twentieth century machine-age style.

Today's railway machinery makes no such decisive and influential impression. When in the 30's the stylists began stuffing steam into streamlined packages, the locomotive had already begun its slide into conformity and oblivion. Defined by the noncommittal contours of its molded envelope rather than the forceful geometry of its basic structure — whether electric, diesel or even steam makes no difference — it became just another powerhead, a little bigger perhaps, but not greatly different from the competitor on the highway, the trailer tractor.

Stu Bryant's Georgian locomotives are among the last of a classic breed. They are also something unique — an indigenous architecture of the Age of Steam.

Richard Janson
The University of Vermont

Preface

THERE IS a plaintive little medley of college songs the bands almost always play at dances for the very young in Virginia. The musicians strike jauntily into the "Tech Triumph" of the Virginia Polytechnic Institute. And the dancing school pupils — handsome, brave and a little self-conscious — begin their cotillion, two by two. Then, with Millerian saxophones and Laninesque rhythm, the band shifts into the catchy airs of "When the line starts to weaken . . . " which is of course "The V.M.I. Swing." Next, a brisk dixieland whack at "The Washington and Lee Swing," followed by a bit of "Rah! Rah! Carolina." This ends with the strains of that most nostalgic of all airs, "Auld Lang Syne," which, although neglected except at the very beginning of the year almost everywhere else in America, is in Virginia "The Good Old Song" of the University of Virginia and is played at football games. The coda is a ragged but energetic recital of the "Are You Ready?" college cheer of the University, if rabid partisans for that institution are on hand — and they nearly always are.

It would take a champion stoic not to be bemused and sentimental at this medley. My memories take the obvious turn at first: they almost always go back to the football Saturdays of boyhood. But then: it seemed that the football stadiums were almost always near the mainlines of my favorite railroads, and, my being a hyper-fanatic railfan, any game was quickly forgotten whenever there was "action" on, say, the Southern Railway or the Chesapeake and Ohio. My reaction may seem curious (and doubtless, to some, murkily psychological), but, really, I sometimes wondered, wasn't the band also playing in cheer for the glorious locomotives of the C.&O. or Southern and not just for the athletes on the field?

Well, they *were* glorious. The locomotives of the nineteen twenties and thirties in the Southern and Southeastern states were imposing and good to look at. They gave the railroads they belonged to color, an air of panache and a rather formidable sense of high quality. People of taste and an eye for line and hue who don't ordinarily *think* much of railroads remember actively the bright splash they made in the Southern landscape. Here hurtled along with crack expresses the arresting passenger steamers of the Southern Railway System, with their apple green sides and gold paint trim. Here were the splendid "Governor", "Statesman" and "General" series of 4-8-4 types for the Richmond, Fredericksburg and Potomac, each with delicate striping in gold lines, and lettering on the tender sides and cab carried out with the care of a fine printer's title page. Here also the blue, old gold, Greek fret decorations and endearing *Gemütlich* of the St. Louis-San Francisco "1500" series 4-8-2 types; jet black, dazzling brass fittings and a patrician countenance in the C.&O. passenger fleet; white trim and the scarlet "Katy" herald on steam power for the Missouri-Kansas-Texas Railroad.

As we think of them now, all the engines of this breed seem to have made up a clear entity in the history of American taste and design—a sidelight, to be sure, but a pungent and memorable one. They flared up in the bright years after World War I. They brought new grace to the old cities of the Southern region, and excitement and a glimpse of the outside world to many an isolated hamlet. They lived until streamlining and the taste for "thirties modern"—that last flare up of the art nouveau movement that critics call "futurism" and that is typified so perfectly in the Chrysler Building of New York City — began to modify some of them. And until the diesel locomotive brought them to an end.

This book attempts to chronicle informally this special species of steamer which, by its atmosphere and patina, seems so justly "The Georgian Locomotive." It illustrates some of the most characteristic specimens — from Northern Virginia to West Texas. It will attempt to put the locomotive in the larger context of the taste of its time. And it tells, if incidentally, of a happy time when steam was still God on American roads and railroading seemed a secure and impregnable business.

Except on the Chesapeake and Ohio, The Georgian Locomotive was never really prepossessing mechanically. Most engines in this category were the comfortably tried and true 4-6-2, 4-8-2 and 2-8-2 types developed over the turn of the century — in sum, the American steam locomotive at one remove from what was to be the apogee of its maturity in the second quarter of the twentieth century. The really great masterpieces of speed, hauling power and high performance in American steam railroading of the 1920-45 period — the imposing Santa Fe 5000's, the Union Pacific 4-12-2's and "Big Boy" articulateds, and the Pennsylvania T-1's — cannot be dealt with here, however interesting they may have been.

And let us be certain to recognize that the South and Southwest had no corner on handsome locomotives in the years 1920-1945. We all cherish memories of the wonderful "Hudsons" of the New York Central, which have justly been called the most beautiful engines in American history. (Who that loved locomotives as a child in the thirties didn't have that Walter Mitty dream of being Bob Butterfield at the throttle of the Central's 5200?) The big Pacific-type engines of the Erie — all black, scarlet, brass-bright and silvered; the aristocratic 1350-series Pacifics of the New Haven (so appropriately assigned the old *Merchants* among other trains); the sparkling Northern Pacific passenger fleet — all had splendid style in livery. But these were isolated instances, and, by and large, locomotives on the big Northern and Western lines — Pennsylvania and Southern Pacific were conspicuous examples that come to mind — were held to a dull standardization in grooming. Certainly the Pennsylvania K-4 Pacific type was a high point in comely locomotive design. But, after all, every K-4 looked exactly like the next one. Even with the Central's Hudsons, a standardized austerity in livery was the mode.

A word about what can fairly be called the aesthetics of locomotive watching. Of course the serious steam locomotive fan has always been the most rigid of purists, the most jealous of connoisseurs. He is rarely prone to allow comparisons of his love with other architectural or artistic creations of any kind, and he shrinks from such a word as "aesthetic." But, nevertheless, the aesthetic comparison is there and deserves to be made.

The steam locomotives of the age just past needed, in their commission to meet high standards of efficiency and capacity, to be pampered with the most complex of auxiliary equipment: reservoirs, pipes, pumps, coils, springs, worms, and levers — so that each was subtle and rich in the architecture of its appliances.

Plans for steam locomotives rarely called for skewed or whimsical lines anywhere. It was circles, segments of circles and triangles that were needed, and these were put to extremely intricate organization. Obviously then the steam locomotive admits of serious comparison with classical architecture. It must be likened to the classical buildings of Greece and Rome and their Italian renaissance, French Louis XIV and English Georgian derivatives, all of which also trade heavily in complicated applications of simple geometric shapes.

In the locomotive, as in the Greek temple or the renaissance villa, some indefinable standard of harmony has to decide whether the parts have come together pleasingly. From one point of view, the beauty of a steam locomotive, when it could be called beautiful, could have been considered more of a miracle than the beauty of a fine renaissance church. For the church was deliberately intended to have grace; it was commissioned on that basis. If the locomotive achieved grace, it was due in part to favorable circumstances (*i.e.*, what had to go into the locomotive to make it work efficiently) and in part to the (largely unconscious) capacity of the designing draftsmen for fine line and agreeable synthesis.

Now The Georgian Locomotive came at a time of sharp readjustment in American building taste. The nineteen tens and twenties rejected the fantasies and free essays in traditional forms — the gingerbreading of renaissance and Gothic architectural styles — that had characterized so much domestic and church building in the 1870-1910 years. And the twenties saw a halt in the movement to a "modern" and truly original architecture, which had begun so brightly with Frank Lloyd Wright and Louis Sullivan during the years at the turn of the century. Now came a new breed of architect: men like Harry McKim, Carrére and Hastings, John Russell Pope, William Adams Delano, A. Stewart Walker and William Lawrence Bottomley reestablished "correct" canons for house building in the traditional renaissance styles. Ralph Adams Cram, that most influential of medievalists; Allen and Collens and James Gamble Rogers set the modes in Gothic — building in the "authentic" late English Gothic vein (usually called "Collegiate Gothic") that produced the Harkness Tower at Yale, the graduate school at Princeton, Union Theological Seminary and many an imposing city church. This was a time when the American of ambition and taste wanted to live amid elegance of an European and traditional sort, even if it had to be reproduced. Certainly it was a time when he was not *afraid* of building elegance — afraid it would label him as ostentatious or undemocratic. He thirsted for what the critic Henry Hope Reed Jr. has called "The Grand Design".

Of course many serious architectural critics deplore the work of these schools; they feel that during this period we should have been going ahead with the new forms developed by Wright and Sullivan and making our own interpretations of the clean new buildings of the Bauhaus designers in Germany. But the revival schools did produce some very carefully worked and attractively proportioned building. And we are surely the richer for having it.

In the South were built the grand neo-Georgian houses of Mr. Bottomley on Monument Avenue in Richmond and Neel Reid's domestic triumphs in the northwest suburbs of Atlanta; the Cram and Ferguson brick Tudor buildings at the University of Richmond, Horace Trumbauer's Gothic Duke University; the grand First Baptist Church series in Georgia, North Carolina and Tennessee; and many a splendid mansion in chaste treatments of the traditional French styles in the suburbs of Dallas and Tulsa. Even railroad stations caught the fervor, and nothing is more characteristic of the revival of building in the correct traditional styles than Mr. Pope's Broad Street Station in Richmond, or the classical Southern Railway stations in Greensboro and (until the last decade) New Orleans. It was on this wave of taste that the Southern and Southwestern roads began a "renaissance" of high style in locomotive grooming.

In the South and elsewhere in the United States, engines of the teens had for the most part been drab — as a clear reaction from the rococo excesses in grooming and style of the diamond-stack locomotives of the nineteenth century. Then after World War I, a return to style, but in a different direction. Grooming was sparkling but not (or not usually) bizarre. The influence of end-of-the-century fire engine livery was readily apparent, and so also that of British locomotive practice in the late nineteenth century,* but the spirit seemed that of Palladian Georgian. Traditional black, "Pullman" green (a sort of olive), bright green, and navy were the basic locomotive colors. Smokeboxes and fireboxes were painted with a smudge-resistant dull gray paint that served as handsome relief to the glossy enamel of boiler and cab. Cab windows, the insides of bells, the lining of numeral plates were often scarlet. The outsides of bells, the rods and levers of "running gear" for the drivers, numeral faces of number plates and, in some cases, air pump cylinders were brass and brightly burnished. Wheel tires and running boards were whitened for accent. On this framework came the variations: striping — often of great delicacy — to simulate Georgian paneling; stylish lettering, sometimes the large, extended-face Bank Modern-like numerals of nineteenth century British practice on tender sides; colorful railway heralds. And then the personal touches that, when management allowed, some engine crews affected: Masonic emblems over the headlight, an engineman's name on the valve gear hangar, stars on cylinder heads and sides, brass or copper strapping on boilers.

All of this came just after an event of extraordinary influence for American locomotive design. This was the United States Railway Administration of American roads during World War I. Frederick Westing in *Trains,* has told how the U.S.R.A. developed a set of designs for American steamers that were superlative — both for their mechanical quality and for their aesthetic perfection. And the U.S.R.A. plans were to dominate locomotive building in North America for the entire decade of the twenties and even then some. Certainly they made for many a fine looking locomotive. It seems worth saying that in almost

*The difference in style between American and British locomotives of the late Victorian period has always seemed remarkable to the writer. Compare the British "Patrick Stirling" (North Eastern Railroad Number 1) with, say, the American "Nathaniel McKay" — both circa 1870. The British engine is superlatively *sheer;* it seems as bereft of "extras" as a rocket. The "Stirling," remember, is contemporary with some of the worst excesses in ornament of British Victorian building and decoration and of the beginning of the Eastlake taste, although it does coincide with the start of Norman Shaw's creditable Queen Anne Revival. The American seems charming but extremely awkward. With the lancet windows of its rather squashed cab, the ornamental ironwork of its headlight, and bolection mouldings applied to its sand and steam domes, it is the perfect accompaniment to the gawky versions of Gothic and Francis I architecture built in this country circa 1870.

THE CLASSIC U.S.R.A. CONVENTIONS: Locomotive 326 of the Georgia Railroad was a perfect example of the United States Railway Administration designs. Identifying points are (1) the multi-bolted smokebox door with its centered headlight and bell mount ("The U.S.R.A. front end"), (2) running boards stepped over the cylinders, (3) neat, unadorned sand and steam domes, (4) gambrel roofed cab, and (5) fabricated (rather than cast) trailer truck. As such the engine represented the farthest point in American locomotive design, circa 1920. Most American locomotives of the post-1920 period were built to some modification of this simple set of patterns.

every case, The Georgian Locomotive was some variation of the U.S.R.A. designs, and some — the Southern and M-K-T Pacifics and almost everybody's switchers — were quite exactly modeled on the government specifications. Even judged as isolated castings and shapings, the components of the U.S.R.A. locomotive were worthy examples of industrial design. Let us cite especially the distinctive smokebox door—that which fans call the "U.S.R.A. front end" — the domes, the cab, the tender of U.S.R.A or U.S.R.A.-inspired steam power.

And then one other fortunate influence in design: just after the U.S.R.A. had ended, the locomotive builders began specifying the truck castings of the General Steel Castings Co., Inc. — the "Delta" trailing (*i.e.*, under the firebox) and tender trucks. The author considers the Delta castings to be extraordinarily fine examples of machine design.

It surprised some of us that the diesel snuffed out the American locomotive as thoroughly, as relentlessly and as quickly as it did. But

xviii

the splendid Southern Ps-4 Pacific types and Frisco 1500's might have been doomed to disappear as such anyway, regardless of whether or not the diesel had come along. For a decisive change in American building taste and industrial design became inevitable as the nineteen thirties wore on, as one of the important results of the famous Museum of Modern Art architectural show of 1932 and other restless aesthetic forces. (It is fascinating to follow the changes in editorial matter and emphasis in *Architectural Forum* over the period 1929-1935 — from Pope-Bottomley Georgian and Cram Gothic to Raymond Hood-Howe and Lescaze modern.) The great era of "correct" period styles in American buildings and interiors (and American locomotive grooming) seemed certain to end.

If the American steam locomotive of the twenties and thirties *sui generis* was a high success in industrial design, the deliberate attempts to streamline her in the later thirties in the South and elsewhere were almost uniformly unhappy. The unconscious tastes of anonymous locomotive draftsmen at Baldwin, Alco, and at the locomotive shops of the railroads themselves, produced far more beauty than the conscious strivings

CHESAPEAKE AND OHIO

THE SHROUDED STEAM LOCOMOTIVE — Chesapeake and Ohio 490 was one of the hundred or so American steam locomotives that were given streamlining or semi-streamlining towards the end of the steam era. The fluted sides and futuristic front-end seem charateristic of the generally mediocre taste shown in these modernizing projects. Workmanship and design in the shrouding seem decidedly inferior. But in the functional parts of the modernization — the alloy rods and trailer truck — design seems of a very high quality. The 490 had been one of the C.&O. F-18 series, with pumps and feedwater heater about the smokebox front.

of such designers as Raymond Loewy and Otto Kuhler to "dress up" the steam locomotive. The jacketing of Southern Railway 1380, of Chesapeake and Ohio 490, of Seaboard 867 and of St. Louis-San Francisco 4-6-2's and 4-8-2's — all with chrome-trimmed shrouds in the high "thirties modern" style — was upsetting to those of us who loved the locomotive in its proper traditional form. The results seemed tawdry and foolish. It was like the Halloween painting-up of some proud hunting hound. Fortunately, the attempts were few; as they went heavily to diesels, the railroads gave up streamlining the steamer. The overdressed bleach-blonde of a locomotive quickly lost the status given it by a railway management conscious of public relations; it was reduced to being just one more unit of motive power pooled in among the conventional steamers.

What would steam have looked like in the sixties? Who knows? Perhaps we are well out of it to be spared the mauve, cream and purple, or the red-and-ochre monster with colossal lettering in Egyptian Bold Extended that might (judging by the diesels of today) have characterized the Pacifics and Hudsons and 4-6-6-4's of the nineteen sixties.

Curiously, one finds here and there a railroad that, even with total dieselization, manages to preserve a bit of the spirit of the twenties and thirties. Thinking of the color of Southern or R.F.&P., we once berated the Illinois Central for its dull standardization. And still we must. But we enjoy any engine terminal today on the I.C. We appreciate it that, as modern as it is under the skin, this road likes to roll them in the old style. Its husky GP's (freight diesels from the Electro-Motive Division of General Motors) work soberly in the traditional black, with big nineteenth century numerals on their flanks. They grind in and out of engine terminals in the old manner — big, dashing, muscular steel steeds. On to the turntable with a convincing banging of wheels against the break in the rails; into the roundhouse . . . . later, out of the roundhouse, smartly up to the sander; then, with an energetic grind, forward to the ready track. Central rackets through the Mississippi hamlets, blowing a big whining whistle that sounds like steam. The road, indeed, very nearly reeks of bituminous coal smoke: you can easily dream of a bank of eight high drivers getting a grip on the rail with a long manifest freight, and six-wheeled "Buckeye" tender trucks clacking over switch points onto the heavy steel of a main line. In this frame of mind, we can almost love the diesel.

But here, now, let us enjoy the engines as they were in the South and Southwest of this country from 1920 on — stylish and proud in their assignments with the best trains. The band is playing "Way Down in Old Virginia . . ." and the Cavaliers may be far behind, but *The Birmingham Special* is marching onto the trestle up there behind the greenest, most polished, smartest Pacific type you've ever seen. . . .

PACIFICUS AMERICANUS — Southern Railway 6686 — a representative of the road's early (1924) series of Ps-4 Pacific types — typified the sharp-featured steam designing favored in the United States. Piping, bolting and efficiency appliances are kept in plain view. About the headlight are the classic Southern eagle and candlesticks.

J. W. TURNIPSEED AND A. H. PEPPERCORN

PACIFICUS BRITTANICUS — The British taste for *sheer* locomotives is perfectly exemplified in former London and North Eastern locomotive 525 (now assigned the Northeastern Region of British Railways). Much of the piping and bolting is concealed beneath the jacket of the engine. This is one of a class of engines inspired by the designs of the great L. N. E. R. builder, Sir Nigel Gresley. Legend has it that it was the green and gold livery of L. N. E. R. that inspired the American Southern Railway to finish its passenger engines in green and gold. A. H. Peppercorn was the builder for this class of British engines.

CHAPTER 1

Eagle Over The Headlight

The Great Days of the Southern in Steam

THE SOUTHERN Railway was a make-believe among steam railroads. Its trains had such fanciful names as *The Crescent Limited, The Bean Man, The Skyline Special, The Spinning Wheel, The Queen and Crescent, The Ponce de Leon.* Its bright green passenger steamers and its black freighters — vivid with gold, silver and scarlet trim — seemed really not quite of this prosaic world; they were high Chippendale with brass eagles, stars on the cylinders, Masonic wheels, polished candlesticks about the headlight, the names of their engineers on the valve gear hanger in gilded Baskerville letters. Southern was, in short, a child's delight — a fantasy that might have lived in some distant Carolingian province, an appurtenance to knights and castles and damsels in distress. It must somewhere have had a branch to the Land of Oz, and Frank Merriwell must have heroically invaded the right-of-way to rescue runaway expresses and win the hearts of station agents' daughters. With the Southern it was always Garden Week in Virginia, April on the Habersham Road, and the Ole Miss game at Tuscaloosa.

In truth there was nothing fantastic about the Southern in steam. It ran trains of modest size behind locomotives of modest size on schedules that were so slow as to be positively *im*modest. In locomotive development, the Southern lagged — complacently happy, it seemed, to leave it for others to carry out the valuable experiments and improvements in the engineering of steam power.

But never mind. The Southern had style — *high* style — and we were all grateful to it. It was as if the carrier summed up all the romantic humors of the region it served. And the Southern's was a *benign* South, the South of Dr. William Alexander Carruther's novels and, in our day, Frances Gray Patton, and not that harsh (if undeniable) South

1

LYNCHBU[RG]

PHOTO BY THE AUTHOR

THE PROTOTYPICAL Ps-4 - Pacific type 6690— all apple green jacketing with numbering and striping in gold leaf paint — was typical of Southern Railway's first-line class of mainline locomotives in the age of steam locomotion just past. Such color and line striping seem highly reminiscent of British railway practice in the 1880-1920 period. Engine 6690, assigned originally to the Alabama Great Southern Division of the Southern, was one of the Ps-4 series built in the mid-Twenties to handle *The Crescent Limited.*

of Mr. Faulkner's fiction or that South unmasked of William Cash's *The Mind of the South.* "The Southern Railway under the absolute monarchy of steam was the most persuasively beautiful carrier I have ever known," wrote David P. Morgan of *Trains* so authoritatively, in a paean to the line some years back. And he spoke for a good proportion of the steam "fraternity."

They say that Fairfax Harrison, the Virginia gentleman-farmer who ran the Southern for most of the teens, twenties and thirties, was responsible for the wonderful green engines. President Harrison, who came to the road as a young solicitor with a Yale-Columbia Law School background, had always been something of a dreamer and scholar when away from the strenuous practical duties his being the head of a large rail system entailed.

In 1913, Harrison had edited for Americans the treatises of Cato and Varro on Roman farm management. This poetically-minded man had seen copies of the writings in a book stall on the Quai Voltaire in Paris, and, as he writes, they had made him think not of olive groves in the Roman campagna, but of "the blue hills of a far distant Virginia where the corn was beginning to tassel and the fat cattle were loafing in the pasture."

There must have been more of the same in 1925 when, at King's Cross Station in London, Harrison saw the Pacific type engines of the London and North Eastern, which had been given almost aero-nautically sleek lines by the line's famous locomotive designer, Sir Nigel Gresley. Each was painted an arresting apple green relieved by gilded lettering and numbering. Harrison must immediately have envisioned such gaily colored steam locomotives as rocketing through his own northern Virginia meadows. At any rate, he ordered a new series of heavy weight 4-6-2 types the Southern was having built — the now-celebrated Ps-4 class — to be given the same green livery.

They must have seemed like vast pieces of French tôleware as they rolled from the erecting halls at the Richmond Locomotive Works, with all the green-enameled sheet metal of their sides decorated with delicate gilded lines and lettering. Indeed, the Southern System 4-6-2's always seemed rather more like possessions than machines. They were antique when brand new.

4

EAGLE OVER THE HEADLIGHT

Harrison had one set of the new Ps-4 types lettered "The Crescent Limited" on their tenders (and it must have been some clever employee's suggestion to make the "C" of "Crescent" into the shape of a half moon). This set of engines was to handle the Southern's premium express—made up entirely of Pullman sleepers, a lounge and a diner — that ran (and still runs as simply *The Crescent*) between New York and New Orleans. Others of the class came to handle *The Royal Palm* (Cincinnati-Florida), *The Birmingham Special*, *The Memphis Special* and *The Piedmont Limited*. The Ps-4 types for the Southern's Cincinnati, New Orleans and Texas Pacific Division — the line that winds through the Smokies between Cincinnati and Chattanooga — gained an extraordinary appearance with their special ducts over the boiler to carry the smoke of tunnels safely away from the engine cab.

The green livery took everyone's fancy along the Southern. It was to become the standard color for all the system's passenger locomotives:

THE C.N.O.&T.P. STYLE — No enthusiast for the Southern would fail to identify this as a passenger steamer assigned the C.N.O.&T.P. Division of the system, which runs through the Cumberland Mountains between Chattanooga and Cincinnati. Those formidable-looking ducts atop the boiler carried dangerous exhaust fumes away from the cab when the engine worked through the many tunnels of C.N.O.&T.P. The delicate twin line striping was always typical of C.N.O.&T.P. practice. So also the broken running boards and looped handrail on the pilot steps.

FROM RICHARD J. COOK; AUTHOR'S COLLECTION

AUTHOR'S COLLECTION; FROM WALTER H. THRALL

THOMAS WOLFE KNEW HER: Apple green Mountain Type 1480 — assigned the Asheville Division of the Southern Railway — could easily have been one of the locomotives Thomas Wolfe was thinking of when he wrote so lyrically of railroads in his novels. Wolfe rode behind other Southern steam power — surely the Ps-4 Pacific types — during his brooding trips across Virginia, the subject of some of his most affecting writings.

FROM ROBERT J. FOSTER; AUTHOR'S COLLECTION

WHEN SOUTHERN "BEEFED UP" ITS SMALLER POWER — a light Pacific type in the gay livery of the Louisville-St. Louis Division. Given a feedwater heater system, single guide crossheads, enlarged sand-dome and considerably enlarged tender, Engine 1234 was made to resemble her heavier and younger cousins, the mainline Ps-4 Pacific types.

FROM ROBERT P. MORRIS; AUTHOR'S COLLECTION

SWITCHER IN THE PASSENGER STYLE — O-6-O type 1653 — given Southern's "passenger" livery: line striping and the letters "Southern" on the tender sides — posed in the yard at the Spencer (N. C.) shops. Her crew has given her an eagle on the smokebox front, a numberplate carrying the emblem of some Masonic unit and brass strapping on the boiler domes.

for the Ps-4 series that had preceded the 1925 batch; the 4-8-2 types handling the Smoky and Cumberland mountain operations; the neat ten wheelers that rolled over the Georgia, Southern and Florida Division; and the tiny American types that worked the Selma, Alabama line.

It had been the Southern's custom — a holdover from the nineteenth century — to offer its engine crews "ownership" of their locomotives* From this inevitably came personal touches in engine decor. Many Southern enginemen were and are Masons and members of other brotherhoods, and the decorative emblems of their organizations became frequent devices used to dress up the steamers. The ornament the Southern is most remembered for is of course the brass eagle — used with the same sense of propriety as the Eagle of the Republic set over the doorway of a New England cottage. The eagle, brass and highly

---

*Connoisseurs found the Southern of a very particular interest because of an extraordinary variety in the *detailing* of its engines. This was because the motive power departments of the system were loosely federated and semi-autonomous, rather than organized by the usual pyramid of executive power coming down from the top. Each shop on the system had its own ideas. Fans loved to note the differences: beautifully "built up" tenders on the Knoxville Division, raised running boards on the Washington Division, "Illinois Central" handrails on the Louisville Division.

HUSKY EASTERN LINES MIKE — Engine 4866 handled heavy-duty freight service on the Eastern (Washington-Atlanta) lines of the Southern. Here she is just fresh from a shopping at Spencer, N. C. — with "running gear" burnished, and wheel tires and running boards whitened.

polished, was most often set over the headlight and flanked by the turned brass rods or "candlesticks" of railroading in the nineteenth century. One recalls seeing the silhouette of an arrowman poised with drawn bow —this again set over the locomotive headlight. Some engines had ornate number plates of sans serif numerals distorted as if they were some fancy, very modern advertising type executed by the Phototype process (serifed numerals, in a normal, rectangular pattern, were "standard" for Southern locomotives). On the Alabama Great Southern Division there rolled a 4-6-2 type carrying the fanciful name "J. W. Turnipseed" on her valve gear hangar. Commemoration of some Alabama folk hero? Indeed no! That was the name of her engineer.

A regional variation on the Southern — with a welded-together cab, big sand dome and neatly built up tender, Consolidation type 677 seemed much like Southern locomotives heavier and later in period. Steam fans can readily identify her as a "Knoxville" (belonging to the Knoxville Division) engine, what with her welded cab, raised cab handrails, and headlight set well below the center of the boiler diameter.

THE GEORGIAN LOCOMOTIVE

We think today of the green Southern passenger locomotive — and particularly the Ps-4 Pacific type — as part of the Southern's Augustan Age, to be remembered along with the double-tracked speedway from Washington to Atlanta,* the olive green string of *The Royal Palm*, and those austere but highly elegant business cars, "The Virginia" and "The Carolina." And let us add the lounge-observation-Pullman car "L. Q. C. Lamar" — named for the enlightened Mississippi statesman of the reconstruction period — always cut in at the tail end of *The Crescent Limited*.

In his poetical autobiography, John Betjeman has told of a favorite Oxford don who toured the English countryside on a bicycle in search of "E. E.," "Dec.," or "West Country Perp" — those quintessentially English abbreviations that tell of various periods of Gothic architecture. It was with some of the same annihilating (to "rational" concerns) passion of lovers of Gothic architecture or medieval church brasses that we steam fans beat the countryside in search of the almost unlimited varieties of the steam locomotive. How true of us that Derby Day in Louisville was memorable not for the horse race or the extraordinary social festivities but because many special trains had rolled in with the week end visitors, and the engine terminals of the town were full of varieties of steam not to be seen there at any other time of the year. "Hudsons are at the Central's terminal," was the cry. "The B.&O. rolled in a big (how we loved to call a locomotive "big"!) rebuilt 'President' series." "There's a Pennsy M-1 with a big tender over at Tenth Street." "The I.C.'s 2499 is in town."

*At the writing, electronic developments in train dispatching, the "Centralized Traffic Control" system, have progressed to a point that the Southern can reduce much of the Washington-Atlanta mainline to a single track — a project being completed in the early nineteen sixties.

And: "The Southern rolled in a special behind Washington Division Ms-4's." Well, the Southern's Ms-4 freighters, built to the heavier United States Railway Administration specifications, were prime hunting on railfan tours. In all his fervor to give the passenger engines style, President Harrison had let his freight engines be — in the old manner: black with scarlet cab windows and tender back heads, and yellow numerals on the tender sides. Perhaps to the serious fan they were even more interesting than the green passenger locomotives. And as for personal touches, the freight hoggers may have had less seniority than their passenger brethren, but they were not to be outdone. *Their* engines were to be noticed, too. Brass got the same rigorous treatment. So did wheel tires and running gear. The result was that the Southern 2-8-2's, 2-8-0's, and even the 2-10-2's and Mallets were some of the most stylish freight locomotives anywhere. Especial care was lavished on the "light" U.S.R.A. 2-8-2's — 4700's on the "mainline"; numbers 6285-6319 for the C.N.O.&T.P. Division; and numbers 6612-6621 for the A.G.S. Division. Crews liked to call them "sport models."

A painful little of the Southern's last thirty years in steam survives. For when the railroad began to complete its dieselization over the years 1950-1955, it scrapped its steam power quietly, quickly and mercilessly. Of the hundreds of locomotives that made up the road's pools of mainline motive power in the thirties, apparently only the 1401 — certainly a worthy enough example of the Ps-4 passenger class — survives. The engine has been carefully sanded and repainted, and moved to a new wing of the Smithsonian Institute in Washington, D. C. It is to be made a public exhibit, starting sometime in late 1962. The old "double" striping of the engine's early days has been restored. And so has the graphite, heat-resistant paint on the firebox sides and smokebox. One hopes that someday a brass eagle will be mounted above the headlight.

As for the Ms-4 heavy Mikado types, none is known to exist today. A few of the heavy, 2500 series 2-8-0's were sent to the Interstate Railroad, a coal carrier in southwest Virginia and eastern Kentucky. Some additional smaller and older engines have been handed down to lines scattered in the Southeast.

What shall we remember of this highly atmospheric Southern Railway System? So many images come back. But I prefer to single out here *The Royal Palm* in steam, as Thomas O. Acree photographed her on the ascending grades just south of Cincinnati on the C.N.O.&T.P. Division. In Acree's picture, it is morning in late April or early May, and the buds are well out on the oaks and maples in our setting — the valleys about Ludlow, Kentucky. The mists are ascending from the Ohio River. The camera is just to the south of a reverse curve Acree particularly loved; the central prop is a pair of immaculate lanes of highly finished trackwork set upon heavy trap rock ballasting — the track laid out on a gentle sine wave. All this is on what Southern "rails" call "Erlanger Hill."

We hear the whistling and racketing exhaust of the locomotive long before the train is in sight. Then, far off on a curve down the line, the train moves into sight — a curling worm: bright green head followed by a long olive green body. It disappears behind the foliage. Then into plain sight on *our* curve. Now you can see that Ps-4 6482 (all the characteristic smoke duct works over the boiler in plain view) is dragging a long train of coaches and Pullmans. She is having to work hard

THE QUEEN BEE AND THE PALM — Engine 6482 — known to fans, if not railroaders, as "The Queen Bee" — was probably the best known passenger engine of the Southern Railway System in steam, and *The Royal Palm* was (and still is) one of the Southern's first line expresses. Here, as photographed by Thomas O. Acree in the thirties, is the *Palm* on Erlanger Hill just south of Cincinnati on a fine spring morning.

AUTHOR'S COLLECTION

on the grade, and showing a good deal of black smoke. Now *going,* as her exhaust overwhelms us and the sound of wheel trucks clack over the rail joints. Now *gone,* as the clicks fade away and the engine whistle reverberates in the next hollow.

I like to think that Claude or Richard Wilson would have taken kindly to this scene (although not Turner; he would have done some highly intellectual "Rain, Steam and Speed" impression). But Southern had no painters — or none that have come forward. And so we must recall *The Royal Palm* through Acree's camera.

CHAPTER 2

The Georgian Locomotive

Steam on the Richmond, Fredericksburg and Potomac Railroad Co.

FOR 125 YEARS, the Richmond, Fredericksburg and Potomac Railroad has steamed northward from Richmond. Its twin lines of heavy steel bisect a region rich in history and architecture and proud of its colonial heritage. The Virginia of the R.F.&P. saw some of the worst fighting during the War Between the States; both Chancellorsville and the Battle of Fredericksburg involved its operations and right of way. Washington called the region along its trackage "home." And so did Lee.

Burdened with all this tradition, the R.F.&P. *should* perhaps be a bit old fogeyish. It is not. The pressures of being heavily trafficked have kept it efficient and up-to-date. That and the pride of the men who run the R.F.&P.

The railroad calls itself "The Capital Cities Route," because from Richmond, capital of Virginia, it runs northward to Washington, D. C. Almost from its beginnings, the R.F.&P. has been blessed at being what railroad traffic men call a "bridge line." It links the metropolitan Northeast with Florida and the coastal South, and much of its traffic is ready-made. A good share of the R.F.&P. passenger business has long been the New York-Florida wintertime traffic, including such famous trains as *West Coast Champion*, *Havana Special* and *Silver Meteor*; these terminate on either the Atlantic Coast Line or the Seaboard Air Line.

However far the trains that use its tracks have reached, the R.F.&P. has, for most of its history, kept its own flavor — the special, English flavor of its parent Virginia. The first locomotives, rails, rolling stock and operating practices were imported from England. Listings of its

13

board of directors have always shown men of obviously Anglo-Saxon descent. Its great passenger station at Richmond, designed by John Russell Pope, is clearly in the English Palladian tradition. The R.F.&P. smacks of boxwood gardens, sash windows, fox hunting and roast beef.

It seems hardly surprising, then, that the road chose the English patterns in grooming its great passenger locomotives of the twentieth century. The twin-line striping, the delicate lettering, the delineation of the R.F.&P. herald all hark directly back to English locomotive livery of the Edwardian period—an art that took much from eighteenth-century styles of coach decoration in England and France. But any literal comparison of the vast, powerful R.F.&P. engines of around 1940 with the rather petit, sporty looking English locomotives of around 1900 would be comical. The R.F.&P. engine seems rather like some sprawling abbey church; the English engine—let us specify a Southeastern and Chatham Class F 4-4-0 or a North Eastern 1400 series—has the air of a smallish but elegant manor church. And it seems curious that R.F.&P. took up the traditional British livery in a period (1925-1945) during which the British themselves had begun to give *their* engines an austere, "modern" livery.

THE GEORGIAN LOCOMOTIVE — Richmond, Fredericksburg and Potomac 613, the *John Marshall.*

Locomotive fans have sometimes complained that the R.F.&P. steam locomotives carry "circus wagon" decorations. Perhaps. I want to say that I remember them as well within the bounds of good taste. Certainly they were imposing—long, long engines, their horizontal lines quite emphasized by the striping. The builder's view (a broadside photograph of an engine just after it has been first painted) of any one of the R.F.&P. 4-8-4's makes me think of Robert Vickry's tempera "Fear," in which the structure in the background seems to be exploding horizontally. And one series, numbers 601-602, offered a most satisfying symmetry, the cylindrical boiler and boxy cab of the locomotive being nicely balanced by the box-shaped coal compartment and cylindrical water tank of the tender.

Am I not just to call the R.F.&P. engine "The Georgian Locomtive"? Surely it expressed all the aspirations to restrained elegance of a Virginia waking from the economic torpors of the War Between the States and the Reconstruction. As we look at a three-quarter view of "The James Madison," one of the big 4-8-4's, we think not of Miss Ellen

THE SOUTHERN "CIRCUS WAGON" STYLE — Gaudy decor was typical among Southern lines in the later days of Steam (above) R.F.&P. 325; (below) Southern Railway 1705, sporting a masonic wheel on the smokebox front and candlesticks flanking the headlight.

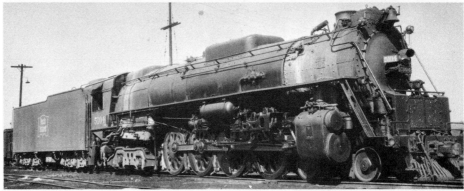

(below) AUGUST A. THIEME, JR.

MIDWESTERN AUSTERITY AND GOOD LOOKS — (above) 2-8-4 No. 709 of the Nickle Plate Road (New York, Chicago and St. Louis), a classic design of the "Super Power" school. (below) 4-8-4 Number 5104 of the Chicago, Rock Island and Pacific.

R.F.&P. (above); AUTHOR (below)

THE GEORGIAN REVIVAL IN RICHMOND LOCOMOTIVE LIVERY AND HOUSES — (above) A builder's view of R.F.&P. 602, the *Governor Thomas Jefferson,* showing striped panels and lines and the railroad herald (inside the diamond on the tender) — all typical livery for the road in the later days of its steam power. The European decorative arts of the eighteenth and nineteenth centuries were the ultimate influence for this livery, but the R.F.&P. "Governors" and other 4-8-4's were built at a time when (nineteen thirties and forties) Virginia was vigorously reviving the Georgian and Colonial arts. (below) A town house in Richmond dating from the early nineteen thirties and reviving late Georgian details of building. William Lawrence Bottomley was architect and the house stands at 2324 Monument Avenue.

Glasgow's tragic and economically down-trodden Richmond of the depression. Here, rather, is the prosperous Richmond of the post-depression and postwar years—the Richmond of chunky gambrel-roofed cottages and Queen Anne brick mansions along Three Chopt Road and in Windsor Farms, of Sweet Briar and the alumni of Saint Anthony Hall, of the summer colony at Gloucester Banks and the Quarry Club. A prosperous, bourgeois, somewhat haughty city set the tone for a prosperous, bourgeois, somewhat haughty railroad.

It was in 1836, with the purchase of seven "Locomotive Engines" from England and one in America, that train operations began for the R.F.&P. As John B. Mordecai, former traffic manager for the road, has chronicled it in his *A Brief History of the Richmond, Fredericksburg and Potomac Railroad*, the engines weighed five tons and cost about $5,000. Mr. Mordecai tells how the first engines were named "Fredericksburg," "Washington," "Potomac," "America" and "Florida." "Later engines were named for Officers and Directors of the Company, for Southern States and for local points on the line."

By 1937 the R.F.&P. locomotive had grown to weigh 220 tons and the railroad was again playing the Name Game. For it was in this year that the really big locomotive came to R.F.&P. with the appearance of the "General" series 4-8-4 types. These were the first of what were to be four orders for long, sleek, locomotive behemoths that pulled their trains from couplings of four large driving wheels and built up the vast quantities of steam they required from fire boxes mounted over four-wheeled trucks. The "Generals" included Lee, Jackson, Stuart and Johnson. In 1938 came the "Governors" (of Virginia), among whom were also four American presidents, Jefferson, Harrison, Monroe and Tyler. The "Statesmen" of 1945 could muster only two presidents—Washington and Madison—but listed such illustrious non-presidents as John Randolph, Carter Braxton and Richard Henry Lee. The remaining batch of big locomotives was the 571-580 series of 2-8-4 types, and, as they were exclusively assigned to freight service, the R.F.&P. forewent naming them.

We remember the "Statesmen" and "Generals" with the excitement of remembering a finely proportioned Georgian or Louis XIV drawing room. There were so many immaculate and tasteful details: the diamond

THE GEORGIAN LOCOMOTIVE

motif that enclosed the R.F.&P. herald on the tender; the four "disk" driving wheels linked by highly polished rods; the square, turret-like cab of each engine with its grand window; the pumps set on the pilot behind bayed-out shields. Each engine seemed fully worthy of the grandee for whom it had been named.

There were several good places to see the R.F.&P. in steam. One was the Ivy City Roundhouse, the engine terminal that serves the Washington, D. C., Union Station. Here one could compare the "Generals" and "Statesmen" with other steam power groomed in the grand tradition — the Southern Railway Ps-4 types, the gleaming C.&O. passenger mainliners, the green and gold B.&O. "President" Pacific types. Or one could go to the "ACCA" engine terminal at Richmond, where the R.F.&P. 4-8-4's waited on the ready tracks side by side with the equally large 4-8-4's in the Atlantic Coast Line 1800 series.

In Richmond, the engines curved into Broad Street Station, in a loop suggesting the layout of a child's Christmas Lionel.

GRAY DAY AT ACCA — Charlie Castner's view of R.F.&P. 606 caught the grimy, oily atmosphere of a gray, foggy, overcast day at a steam engine terminal. The locomotive is just in to the "ACCA" engine terminal at Richmond after a run with an express from Washington, D. C., and the hostler atop the boiler is just about to refill the sand dome with sand.

CHARLES B. CASTNER

AUGUST A. THIEME, JR.

WALKIN' THE DOG — 2-8-4 type 576 at speed with a long manifest freight on the R.F.&P. north of Ashland, Virginia. The view was taken in 1948 a few years before total dieselization on the railroad.

But I prefer to remember the engines as they were at speed—though for the R.F.&P. speed was always less than 71 miles per hour. Despite its splendid roadbed and long lines of tangent or straight trackage, the road chose to limit its engines to 70 m.p.h and, accordingly, equipped them with governors. Well, 70 is a respectable enough figure with a load of 15 or so Pullman cars; at any rate, the illusion of speed was there.

Let us go back for a minute to the years immediately following World War II. The scene is Ashland, a college town some 15 miles north of Richmond, where the railway cuts straight through a small station with twin lines of platforms. We see far down the tracks to the south a dot of smoke. The train comes, on, on. We can see the tender weaving and bucking, so much that it seems as though it will surely drag the engine from the track. Then nearer, gleam of headlight, bell and silver paint of the bottom rib of the pilot. She's on us, drivers rattling like the sound of a steam roller on concrete pavement. *By* us. Then coaches clattering through—the "rack, rack, rack" of six-wheeled trucks and the "rack, rack" of four-wheeled trucks. Then marker lamps pierce the station and the sounds recede—the sounds of American railroading at its apogee.

Many of us who collect antiques and cherish old houses in this country do so because we feel such a terrible isolation from the spiritual and cultural riches of Europe. And we go on collecting and enjoying them and seeing in them the link with European taste and craftsmanship, whatever be the pressures to the contrary and no matter how often we are called "old hat" and admonished to "go modern" and "live in the spirit of the times." The admonishments matter little to us; we know that we, at least, don't find nourishment in the various styles of the modern.

If this longing for European grandeur can explain the Georgian period of the R.F.&P.—its elegant locomotives and classical railway station at Richmond—what explains its present style? Richmond has continued with the taste for the Queen Anne and the Georgian. Houses and even public buildings are still built of red brick and clapboard, with blinds and sash windows. But when the diesel appeared in the

BUCKEYE STEEL CASTINGS

RAILWAY ABSTRACT ART: Locomotive and Tender Truck Castings — (above) Six-wheeled "Buckeye" trucks such as these were used on tenders for the 570-series 2-8-4's of the Richmond, Fredericksburg and Potomac. (below) The casting pictured houses wheels for a "Delta" trailing truck carried by the 4500-series of 4-8-4's for the St. Louis-San Francisco. Both suggest certain sculptures of the twentieth century — notably works of Jacques Lipchitz and Raymond DuChamp Villon.

GENERAL STEEL INDUSTRIES

1940's, the R.F.&P. chose to give up the traditional airs of its parent city. The style of its stainless steel passenger cars and its present locomotives seem no more distinctive than that of the facade of a chain motel.

TWO VERSIONS OF THE F-19 PACIFIC TYPE: C.&O.'s BAROQUE MASTER-PIECE — Graceful and a little monstrous both, this was Chesapeake and Ohio's premium passenger locomotive of the 1926-35 period. (above) Pictured in the early thirties — with stars on the cylinder heads, polished air pumps and bell, lacquered eagle on the feedwater heater header (ahead of the smokestack), and cylindrical "Vanderbilt" tender carrying a signboard for *The George Washington* express — awaits a turn with the *George*. (below) In the mid forties, 493 is pictured at Cincinnati, still handsomely groomed but with a somewhat more austere livery. A high capacity rectangular tender has been substituted for the cylindrical one of the earlier view.

CHAPTER 3
The F-19
And Some of her Cyclopean C.&O. Sisters

LIKE THE facade of some remote Jesuit church in Sicily or Mexico —gilded, late in period and a little overdone—the great passenger locomotives of the Chesapeake and Ohio Railroad put forward a baroque front for the world to see, admire, accept or reject. This image that the C.&O. engines cast — employing as it did some increment of effeteness — was never entirely adequate to the quality of the railroad. For the C.&O. has in our time been a blue-chip property — a well-managed, profitable, solid, vigorous firm that paid its dividends well and satisfied its shippers. It may not be saying too much to assert that C.&O. has consistently been one of the *best* railroads in the world; certainly it has consistently been one of the most *enterprising*.

What the baroque passenger locomotives of the road — efficient and stylish both — did perhaps accurately symbolize was that the C.&O. of the 1920-1940 period was very much two disparate things. On the one hand, it was the highly efficient conveyor belt, the hauler of huge trains of coal from the West Virginia massif to the ship-loading terminals at Hampton Roads and the Great Lakes. That side of the carrier was reflected in superlatives — especially in motive power. Unlike other lines in the South and Southwest, it could boast of abundant "mosts" and "biggests". It had the *biggest* 2-10-4's, the *most* variety in wheel arrangements, the *largest* firebox on wheels, the *most* powerful Hudson types, the *heaviest* Pacific types, the *first* Mountain types, the 2-8-4 with the *greatest* tractive effort rating.

But on the other hand, Chesapeake and Ohio was anything but the impersonal purveyor of bigness. It was, indeed, highly class conscious and something of a social snob. And C.&O. could hardly have been otherwise. Wasn't it truly "George Washington's Railroad"? (Its route

THE *GEORGE* AT SPEED — Pacific type 481, her grooming down a bit because of the exigencies of World War II, gets a fast wheel on *The George Washington* passenger limited south of Alexandria, Virginia — in 1944, late in the days of steam.

follows the canals the young Washington had layed out in the eighteenth century. Didn't it begin on one leg in Virginia's Peninsular — rich, rich in historical association — and on the other in the posh Northern Virginia horse country. It ran through aristocratic Richmond, through Keswick, Charlottesville and Farmington, through Staunton and then (our conveniently skipping the West Virginia coal fields), the Kentucky blue grass country and Louisville. C.&O. was the line that built the Greenbriar Hotel at White Sulphur Springs ("The White") and it also served Hot Springs. It rolled its patrons in heavyweight, all-steel passenger equipment it called "Imperial Salon Cars" — coaches, parlor cars and diners on six-wheeled trucks. It named its trains *The George Washington*, *The FFV* ("Fast Flying Virginian" in C.&O.'s translation) and, inevitably, *The Sportsman*. Historian Charles W. Turner caught some of the line's individuality when — in his history of the C.&O. — he called it "Chessie's Road" for the luxury-loving kitten that has so often been a feature of C.&O. advertising.

26

It is curious that the truly formal and elegant days of Chesapeake and Ohio in this century came during the depression of the thirties — a time in which the most influential forces for taste in this country, especially the Museum of Modern Art and its critics, were directing that we move in other and more "functional" directions. For C.&O. moved in the same (to its proponents) delicious cultural lag that has produced the powerful Queen Anne-Williamsburg revival in Virginia suburban building and decoration. Not for C.&O. were to be the moves to lightweight, streamlined futuristic trains — the Union Pacific *City* trains and the Burlington *Zephyrs* of the mid thirties. C.&O. would roll its patrons in true Georgian (or Edwardian) style, and its locomotives would be complementary to this taste —*just* so.

Although it may not have been C.&O.'s best-known steam locomotive, the F-19 Pacific type was surely the most representative of the road's elegant age. The F-19's had really dated from the mid-twenties — from the days when the Van Sweringen brothers of Cleveland had controlled the C.&O. as part of the rail empire they deftly acquired, managed ambitiously, and finally lost. The F-19 Pacifics were always startling — a disciplined jungle of gaunt shapes rather like some device in a Piranesian prison — what with their feedwater heaters ahead of the stack; their massed display of air pumps, bell, headlight, numeral plates and smokebox door crowded about the smokebox front. The analogy to the facade of a baroque church seems irresistable.

Each engine had a long, odd shaped tender consisting of a boxlike coal bunker set before a cylindrical water tank — that shape that railroaders have always called the "Vanderbilt" tender, since such a design had been specified for locomotives on railroads of the Vanderbilt group in the early part of the century. The F-19 was a giant among Pacific types — one the heaviest locomotives of that wheel arrangement ever built* — and it was designed for very high capacity service, handling heavy trains over rough terrain at good speeds.

But it was not until the depression that the C.&O. truly made "circus wagons" of the big F-19's, which were then assigned to *The George Washington* and the new expresses that line created in the thirties, *The*

*Engines of its sister series, the 480-series F-18 locomotives, were *the* champion heavyweights among Pacific types.

WEARING GEORGE'S CAMEO — This was the C.&O. front end of the early thirties: highly polished pumps on the smokebox, bell "up front," headlight on the pilot, burnished cylinder heads. Because the locomotive handled the express, *The George Washington,* it carried the cameo of the President on its front end.

28

Sportsman (1930) and *The FFV* (1932). In this period the engines were kept highly polished and given nickled stars on the cylinder heads. The alloy jackets of their air pumps were given a high sheen, and eagles were lacquered on the feedwater heater header. Engines handling *The George Washington* sometimes carried a cameo of President George himself atop the smokebox front.

Chesapeake and Ohio made all this the basic style for its heavy road locomotives in the 1930-35 period; the big Pacific types built prior to the F-19 series, 4-8-2's, 2-8-2's and even the big Mallet compounds all had the same arrangement of many fittings up on the smokebox front. To a child, the F-19's and other C.&O. "pumps-in-front" locomotives always seemed at first a little menacing, and then irresistibly mag-netic — the eagerly-sought diamonds in the gem collection that was every C.&O. engine terminal.

With the coming of the J-3 4-8-4's for passenger service — this was in 1935 — the C.&O. changed its style in motive power rather sharply. Here was a cleaner, more stream-styled engine than the F-19's and contemporaries of the previous decade. And bigger and incredibly long. The J-3's (C.&O. called them "Greenbriar" types in honor of its famous resort hotel) were really much larger versions of the beloved and widely-admired New York Central Hudson types, and they had some of the same good looks as the N.Y.C. engines. Here was the neat, post-U.S.R.A. cab that Lima and Alco had often favored for steam freight power, and the enlarged "U.S.R.A. front end". Air pumps were lowered to the engine pilot and set behind neat shields. The headlight, first centered on the smokebox door, was later lowered to a spot about a yard above the pilot, an arrangement long C.&O.'s practice for heavy road power. C.&O. put them to work handling the blue ribbon expresses over the Charlottesville-Charleston grades. All were given the old splendid livery — the white trim, silvered smokebox, gilded lettering. The road named each for a Virginia statesman (*e.g.*, "Patrick Henry", "Thomas Jefferson"). I don't forget the excitement of waiting on a hillside one May night at Goshen, Virginia, in the Appalachain Moun-tains for the 601 and 602 to storm the long curve and grade through the station with the steel cars of *The George Washington*.

TWENTIES BAROQUE — Pacific type 474 displays smart black, gold and white livery, a cylindrical "Vanderbilt" tender and many polished appliances about the smokebox front. Note the cast "Box Pok" drivers — an addition of the thirties.

TWO STAGES OF C.&O. STYLE

THIRTIES CLASSICAL — "Greenbriar" type 600 — the "Thomas Jefferson" — was characteristic of the cleaner locomotive designing of the thirties — with air pumps set on the pilot behind neat shields, and a rectangular tender built to follow the lines of the locomotive.

FROM WALTER H. THRALL;
AUTHOR'S COLLECTION

HOUSECLEANING DAY FOR "PATRICK HENRY" — A hostler shines up the name plate "Patrick Henry" for Chesapeake and Ohio 601, a class J-3 4-8-4 type of the mid thirties assigned to handle the important C.&O. expresses over the Virginia-West Virginia mountains. Such careful grooming was characteristic of the road in the twenties and thirties. Note the "simplified" front end: pumps on pilot behind shields and headlight centered on the smokebox front — this in marked contrast to the cluttered arrangement of earlier C.&O. engines.

I am afraid that in the last days of the J-3's (the early fifties), C.&O. let maintenance slip and the engines were often grimy and the brass name plates allowed to become obscured.

A word about C.&O's last projects in steam road power, the J-3a 4-8-4's and the L-2a 4-6-4's. These engines took the road quite well out of the "Walscheart valve gear, 73-inch-drivers" motive power levels of the Post-World War I period. To be sure, both the J-3a's and L-2a's retained something of the old C.&O. *hauteur*. They were indisputably thoroughbreds. Each featured a snugly built in, rather battleship-like cab, exotic poppet valve gear (which looked so deceptively simple from the exterior of the locomotive), and heavy "solid" pilot. They were huge, highly-developed, highly efficient steamers — but not so efficient that they couldn't be overwhelmed in the fifties by another form of locomotion. Here, in a last few halcyon years before diesels took over on the C.&O., was a glimpse of what might have been the steam power of a missile age — tall, compact locomotives that always seemed a little over-simplified. Some of the piping and appliances of normal locomotives seemed to have disappeared from their boiler tops. Indeed, the J-3a 4-8-4's and L-2a 4-6-4's make the viewer think of the cleaned up classical architecture of Sir Edwin Lutyens's Viceroy's House at New Delhi or Bertram G. Goodhue's State Capital at Lincoln, Nebraska.

Perhaps the L-2a was the absolute culmination of the American steam passenger locomotive. It had the finest mechanical niceties — poppet valves, lightweight running gear, roller bearings, "solid pilot", cast engine bed. If not the most powerful nor yet the fastest American passenger locomotive, it may well have been the most efficient. And aesthetically, it simply had no equal among its immediate American contemporaries. Its simple, compact, flowing lines put it in the class with the French CC 7100 electrics and the post-World War II Peppercorn and Thompson Pacific types built for the former London and North Eastern line.

A trifle too sleek and cleaned up for the traditional coach and Pullman equipment of the twenties, the "Imperial Salon" equipment, the L-2a engines yet seemed a little too gray and conventional for the gleaming new streamlined passenger equipment that now accompanies the diesel locomotives.

FROM C. W. WITBECK; AUTHOR'S COLLECTION

THE HUDSON TYPE *BIEN FAIT* — Intimations of what might have been the loco-motives of the 1960's are given in this view of 4-6-4 type 305 — compact, extremely heavy, utilitarian and possessed of a multitude of efficiency devices.

Here a vignette of steam days on the C.&O.: Came Christmas shopping time and the road brought some of its mainline passenger style to the James River Sub-Division — the water-level freight line that follows the James and tributaries from Clifton Forge through the Blue Ridge Mountains and the Piedmont to Richmond. A gas electric car and lightweight trailer were ordinarily sufficient to handle the modest mail, express and passenger traffic to and from the villages along the river. But in December, the Christmas mail and express traffic grew to a tonnage that got well beyond the capacities of the wheezy gas cars. Then the foreman of engines would assign a steamer to the service.

I think of an icy but entirely sunny December in the mid forties at Reusens, an industrial hamlet near Lynchburg on the James River line. The roundhouse at Clifton Forge has assigned the 483, a heavyweight F-18 Pacific type, to the passenger train, which consists of three heavy all-steel cars riding on six-wheeled trucks — a mail and baggage, a "combine", and a coach. The train is in the "hole" for a merchandise freight so long that it can't be accomodated in the local siding. The 483's hogger moves his train slowly forward on the siding, awaiting sight of the caboose and the tail end of the freight. Then he sees it:

33

"whooooomp . . . whoomp . . whomp . *whomp.* thwack, thwack, thwack, *thwackthwack,* whompwhomp-whompwhompompomp — the 483's sounds were the quick and incisive exhausts of American single-expansion engines (European engines are often "compound" expansion — use their steam twice — and have muddy, slushy exhausts). The 483 whistles for a crossing up the line — a deep, mournful minor chord that reverberates in infinite regression up among the stoves of the blast furnaces at Reusens. The getaway is quick: in a minute the engine has whipped off the siding onto the mainline, and then the tail end of the third car has swung out of sight up above the hydro-electric dam at Reusens.

To Holcombe Rock, to Waugh, to Snowden, to Big Island, to Balcony Falls, to Greenlea, to Irongate; then back to Six Mile Bridge, to Walker's Ford to Warminster, to Bremo Bluff, to Westham this stylish little consist steamed — the flower and fruit of the old Van Sweringen rail empire come to the Blue Ridge fastness and the Piedmont meadows in Virginia.

As we remember her, F-19 was really a bit of a *fondant* among steam locomotives: perhaps she and her sisters were always rather too lush for American tastes. Certainly the paradoxical taste she represents — black rectitude relieved by the brass-bright sybaritic — has become out of date in this country. Who cares for such things these days in our country? A few lovers of antique automobiles and collectors of old French ormulu; New Englanders who reproduce salt box houses; Virginians who reproduce Queen Anne cottages in brick and clapboard. It's all too expensive, too hard to keep clean, requires too much explanation. Bland colors and plastic materials are much more comfortable. Leave for albums and anthologies the bothersome Georgian forms.

Chesapeake and Ohio today? The old, massive signal bridges and heavy track emplacements of its elegant earlier years are still there. But the style of its railroading is quick-to-the-minute, up to date: Centralized Traffic Control, "piggybacking" of truck trailers and, at the writing, some highly ambitious merger talk are all much a part of the present day C.&O. The swashbuckling days of the virtuoso financier Robert F. Young ("A hog can cross the country without changing trains, but *you* can't!") have receded, but the road can boast "C.&O.

For Progress" with justice. Its dark blue and yellow Electro Motive diesels and cabooses are deceptively gay, for they roll their long freights with a somber efficiency. The once proud *George Washington* must now, in the interests of keeping costs to competitive levels, haul along "cuts" of piggyback flatcars loaded with truck trailers.

No more the old aristocratic pretensions. Gone forever the old style of Imperial Salon Cars and Pacific types with polished air pumps.

AUGUST A. THIEME, JR.

SOUTH FROM RICHMOND I — Atlantic Coast Line 4-6-2's 1672 and 1562 get a wheel on a train of empty "reefers" bound for the fruit packers of Georgia and Florida.

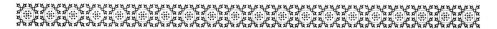

CHAPTER 4

Steam On The Coast Line

And The Seaboard

IN THE opening scene of Hamilton Basso's novel *The View from Pompey's Head*, the hero is returning to his Southern city after an absence of 15 years. Anson Page has ridden for an afternoon and a night on a Pullman after leaving a New York raw and icy in late winter. A porter wakens Page just before daybreak, for he must leave the train at 5:45. The description of Page's first sight of his native district is quite affecting: from the train he can see in the dim light moss-hung live oaks, tulip

SOUTH FROM RICHMOND II — Seaboard Air Line 263 heading a Florida-bound express south from the Union Station at Richmond (shown in background).

trees, red buds in bloom, a muddy tidal creek and a turpentine camp. The reader is immediately confronted with the whole sunny, marshbound aspect of the Southeastern coast, for one of the virtues of *The View from Pompey's Head* is that it is a remarkable travel book.

Mr. Basso's porter says something that makes it clear that Pompey's Head is distinct from Savannah, well below Charleston, and not Beaufort or Brunswick either; and I have heard the novelist explain that his mythical city is an amalgam of all these. But I persist in thinking that Page is really returning to Savannah and that he has perhaps ridden over the Seaboard Air Line's carefully kept mainline steel from Richmond, through North Carolina, Columbia and the lower part of South Carolina. And that he has ridden behind an M-2 4-8-2 with a fast hogger at the throttle, and that his Pullman was part of the consist of *The Southern States Special*.

"*Silver Meteor*" . . . "Q-3 Mikes" . . . "ACCA Engine Terminal" . . . "C.T.C. to Hamlet" . . "P-5a Pacifics" . . "*West Coast Champion*" — to

37

SEABOARD AIR LINE

HOW THEY "UPGRADED" THE SEABOARD M-2's — (above) Seaboard Air Line 237 as built, with small Vanderbilt tender. (below) An engine of the same class was equipped with a larger tender for long distances between watering and refueling, and feedwater heater (ahead of the stack), an efficiency device which pre-heated water from the tender before it entered the boiler tubes. Other typical rebuilding projects to improve locomotives in the thirties and forties included improved crossheads, roller bearings, lightweight side rods to decrease "dynamic augment" or rail pound, and enlarged fireboxes for greater horsepower.

AUGUST A. THIEME, JR.

the knowledgeable these words and symbols all suggest Seaboard Air Line Railway Co. and Atlantic Coast Line Railroad Co. For most people, of course, Seaboard and Coast Line inevitably mean Florida and winter sunshine. I can't hear mention of either without thinking of the excitement of the trip South in late winter. First, the midnight change of trains at Petersburg, Virginia, still frozen in early March. Then the quickening ride over the flatlands of Southside Virginia toward North Carolina. On in the night toward Georgian New Bern, Wilmington and then Charleston, with its beguiling echoes of late-Stuart England, colonial Barbados and seventeenth-century France. Then through the incomparable scenic variety of the barrier-island country of lower South Carolina, through Beaufort to Savannah.

Florida and its fabled resorts are beyond Savannah, but, as before, I want to single out what is perhaps the most attractive city in this whole region: one could go on at length about the pleasures of Savannah — the shady, romantic squares, the rich inventory of domestic and ecclesiastical architecture, the unusual light, which more than in any other part of North America seems truly Mediterranean.

But all this has little to do with the locomotive. What I mean is this: the "stub end" Union Station at Savannah has always, it seems to me, been the focal point for train operations on both the Seaboard and the Coast Line, though neither line maintains shops or main offices here. In Savannah, both lines converge squarely at mid-point, having entangled each other like grapevines south from Richmond and north from Tampa and southern Florida.

The Seaboard and Coast Line had the Union Station to themselves; here, beyond the spacious, but grimy Jacobean station building, one could go out to the platforms and compare meticulously the locomotives of the two railroads — Coast Line's engines extravagant in their striped livery and aluminum paint, and Seaboard's rather old fashioned, with numerals on the tender sides and the railroad herald up on the cab.

February 1938 would have been perfect to watch steam at Union Station, Savannah. Winter traffic to and from Florida is at its seasonal peak, trains are still the prime means of long-distance overland travel, steam still handles the big passenger runs, and the A.C.L. is just breaking in its new 1800 series of 4-8-4's.

39

ATLANTIC COAST LINE

BIG POWER ON THE COAST LINE — This was the prototype locomotive of the Atlantic Coast Line 1800 series, the only essay the road ever tried in high capacity steam power. Several features were unusual for railway practice in the South, notably the cast steel pilot with its "drop" coupler (which could fold down into the pilot member) and the eight wheeled trucks of the tender. Such engines handled the most important passenger trains and the fastest freights during the years immediately before World War II.

On this particular February day, Savannah is sunny-bright but suffers from an unusual cold snap, and the wind has a sharp, cutting bite. Steam drifts down from boiler tops in evanescent wisps, and switchmen and brakemen wear heavy outer coats with upturned collars. In early afternoon there has been a lull in activity at the station. But toward 3:45 a grimy Seaboard F-7 switcher moves onto the lead to the express car tracks. It couples onto a long Baltimore and Ohio baggage car, the engineer hooks back the reverse lever, and the engine puffs forward beyond a switch stand, slowing up with an anguished rattle of brake shoes. Bell ringing, the 0-6-0 starts back again — now pushing the baggage car. Now something is moving toward the station on a nearer track. A long express is backing in, so close that the motions of the conductor on the rear vestibule can easily be seen as he guides the train with air signals to the engineer. The train is *The Robert E. Lee* of the S.A.L. and a large sign, or "drumhead," on the rear platform advertises the fact. More than twenty cars are in the consist, including two sumptuous business cars and, closer to the head end, some older wooden coaches that serve as Jim Crow cars, for this is still the day of segregation on Southern passenger trains. Two beautifully shopped Seaboard M-2 Mountain-type engines are handling *The Robert E. Lee*. Both have the big Vanderbilt tenders on six-wheeled trucks — a frequent adjunct of these engines during the later years of their service.

The Robert E. Lee does not stop for long: it is soon moving off for Florida. But it is hardly gone when the end of an observation car moving in toward the station announces the arrival of another passenger train. This is *The Havana Special* of A.C.L., en route to Miami, and it is fully as long as the *Lee*. On the head end: one of the A.C.L. 4-8-4's.

This rush of express trains and steam power will continue through the late afternoon and early evening. The southbound *New York-Florida Limited* of S.A.L. and the northbound *Gulf Coast Limited* of A.C.L. will be in and out. There will be a tandem of A.C.L. 1500-series Pacific types. Perhaps a Seaboard Q-3 Mike will lumber in with the motor train from Montgomery, the gas-electric motor car having broken down. There will be more Seaboard Mountain types and more Coast Line 4-8-4's.

Locomotives on the Seaboard and Coast Line were not superlative; their engines don't flash in the memory as do C.&O.'s or Frisco's. The Coast Line relied heavily on small versions of the Pacific type for both freight and passenger service, and its most memorable machines in this class were surely the P-5a series. These were built in 1918 under the United States Railway Administration. The A.C.L. 2-8-2's were generally older and smaller engines, and in the later years of steam were not classed as first-line power. The road operated a series of heavy 2-10-2's for "drag" freight service. Then, toward the end of the steam era, the A.C.L. made one experiment with really powerful locomotives — the R-1 4-8-4's (numbers 1800-1811), which were fast but somewhat ponderous machines. I have chased an 1800 in a convertible north of Hardeeville, S. C., where the Coast Line's double-tracked mainline follows U. S.

SWITCHING POWER IN THE SOUTHEAST — (above) Seaboard Air Line 1118 in the modified light U.S.R.A. design. The radar-like dome ahead of the stack housed the mechanism for the "front end" throttle. (below) Atlantic Coast Line 1220 and the U.S.R.A. 0-8-0 design.

Highway 17. The 4-8-4 was hauling at least 100 cars of Florida perishables, but it easily outdistanced me.

The Seaboard's stable of coal-burning locomotives seemed cleaner and wirier—generally more interesting. I still marvel that the lightweight M-2 Mountain types managed all of the pulling they did, keeping up schedules with long sections of Florida-bound expresses. And the Q-3 Mikes seemed almost like branch-line power, "slim-boilered," as train journalists like to say, with small tenders, and with air pumps that stuck out from their places atop the skinny smokebox front. But the Q-3's handled red ball freight nicely on a line notable for the dispatch of its freight service. Of course, it is not always remembered that the Seaboard had some fairly large steam power in its 2-6-6-4's, which were built for hauling long freights at swift speeds.

What were the design antecedents for the admirable American steam locomotives of the twenties and thirties? Not the gaudy diamond-stacked American locomotives of the eighties and nineties. Yet surely *some* aspect of American design in the nineteenth century. In his books

42

AUGUST A. THIEME, JR.

THE WIRY SEABOARD Q-3 — Although its boiler seemed small and its dimensions generally puny, Seaboard 355 handled fast merchandise freight for that road. Air pumps on the smokebox front gave the locomotive a scare-crow aspect.

THE STOCKY COAST LINE Q-1 — The 2-10-2 wheel arrangement usually meant long freights at slow speeds, and such was the usual work for Atlantic Coast Line 2006. The locomotive displays typical livery for the line in the late thirties and forties: the line stripe bisecting the tender horizontally, herald in the center of the tender, a striped panel on the cylinder. Wheels were often picked out in aluminum paint, as in this picture.

J. B. ALLEN

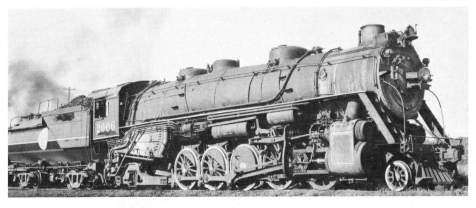

Space, Time and Architecture and *Mechanization Takes Command*, Sigfried Giedion has noted the admiration of Europeans in the nineteenth century for American machines. Of an exhibition in 1851 he records that European observers "were astonished by the simplicity, technical

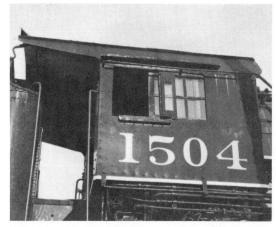

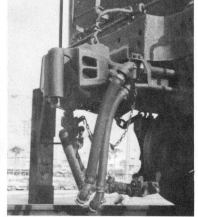

The cab (1)   The coupling (1)

THE ANATOMY OF STEAM

All photographs by the author; numbers represent as follows: (1) *Atlantic Coast Line 1500-series 4-6-2;* (2) *Virginia Blue Ridge Railway 0-6-0* (*ex-War Department*); (3) *Louisville and Nashville light 4-6-2;* (4) *Chesapeake and Ohio 2-8-4.*

The running gear (1)

The domes (2)

The eccentric (3)

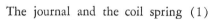

The journal and the coil spring (1)

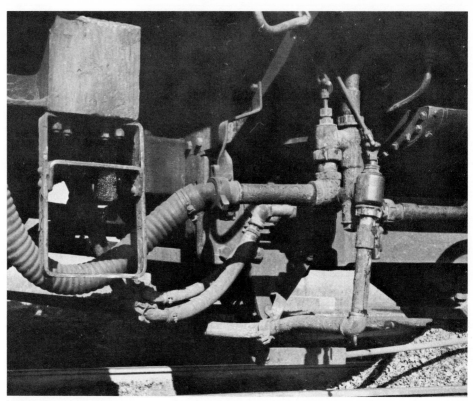

The connection (2)

The front end (1)

The pilot truck and the pump (4)

correctness and sureness of shape revealed" by American tools and machines. He cites from 1875 another visitor's remark on "the beauty of form in which the Americans cast their tools and machinery." And Professor Giedion suggests the influence of our railway design generally when he recalls that the French had an epithet, "the Pullman Style," for our manufactures of the nineteenth century. But I can hardly believe that Giedion thinks of our locomotives of the sixties, seventies and eighties as superior in any way to the locomotives Patrick Stirling was designing in England in the late Victorian period.

It was not really until the end of the nineteenth century that the American steam locomotive showed aesthetic superiority. Locomotive 999 and her sister machines, used on the expresses of the old New York Central and Hudson River Railroad, were incomparably beautiful in their day — not only for the grace of their almost unbelievably lanky proportions, but also for the tasteful script lettering that went into their livery.

Our superiority continued up through the twenties, thirties and early forties. But Europe seems to have taken the lead since 1945. Now that the Chesapeake and Ohio L-2a Hudson types have been scrapped, we have nothing to compare with the finest of European design. Our best today — the Electro-Motive GP series of diesel units — falls far behind the best of England and France. The Thompson and Peppercorn Pacifics for the Eastern Region of British Railways and the "Britannia" Pacifics for the whole British system represent a level of designing that American locomotive and car makers seem to have lost. Is this because, as James Marston Fitch shrewdly suggests about American automobiles, our locomotive designers suffer from pressures to follow surveys and market analysis and have foregone the personal encounter with client and consumer?

In France, a railway system traditionally operated with atrociously ugly locomotives now benefits from electric engines of superlative lines and workmanship. And Professor Fitch cites the high quality of imagination and skillful metalwork that have gone into the latest locomotives and rolling stock for the Italian State Railways.

There are observers who feel that 1918 and the advent of the U.S.R.A. engines represented the high point for locomotive design in this country. In Jacksonville, Florida, the enthusiast can find a perfect example of the American steam locomotive of circa 1918-20. There, displayed in the plaza beside the new, hotel-like headquarters of the A.C.L., stands one of the company's U.S.R.A. Pacific types outfitted in its original livery. The engine is really an astonishing survival of its period: it has undergone very little rebuilding or modification since its manufacture in 1918. I say "astonishing," for engine 1504 served the A.C.L. right up until 1950, straight through three decades of almost continuous development in American steam power. Most other engines built in the twenties were subsequently given heavy rebuilding: enlarged tenders, feedwater heaters, "disk" drivers and a multitude of other efficiency devices. These modifications were for the most part carried out at the expense of the good looks of the engine concerned.

At any rate, A.C.L 1504 stands on a short span of track, conveniently raised so that the valve gear piping is just above eye level and can be examined closely. Here you can see the ingenious and beautiful layout of the Baker valve gear system; and the complex piping to carry fuel, electricity, compressed air, smoke, water, steam, sand, and signals about the engine and tender.

Although 1504 represents a level of technology long since outmoded, the engine is still to be admired. As a machine it seems fully *shibui* — as much so as anything of American design can fulfill the meaning of the Japanese word that suggests balance, restraint, elegance and strength. The engine is complete and satisfying in itself, requiring no Reginald Marsh or Lyonel Feininger to depict it in some artistic trope. As Aldous Huxley has written (and he was not discussing machinery as favorably as I), " . . . a machine is, after all, in itself a work of art, much more subtle, much more interesting, from a formal point of view, than any representation of the machine can be. In other words, a machine is its own highest expression and merely loses by being simplified and quintessentialized in a symbolic representation."

The gallery of photographs of 1504 accompanying these pages attempts to suggest the many aesthetic accomplishments to be found in the locomotive.

Certainly, A.C.L 1504 illustrates perfectly the first-rate designs of the draftsmen for the United States Railway Administration. The sand and steam domes seem to be perfectly placed. The smokebox casting and bolt arrangement are flawless. The cab has just the right proportions.

We know just *who* was responsible for the U.S.R.A. designs. But we don't know *why* the U.S.R.A. designs were to become as pleasing as they did. So very little information seems to have survived on this phase of the U.S.R.A. engine projects.

If we are lucky, the good design for which Professors Giedion and Fitch so ably campaign may return to the American railroads. And the Coast Line and Seaboard — merged or apart — may again have locomotives and rolling stock worthy of the lovely coastal lands they serve.

CHAPTER 5

Motive Power Elegance

In Georgia, in Alabama, in Tennessee, in Kentucky

WHAT ARE your railway superlatives? A Nigel Gresley Pacific type fresh from a shopping at Doncaster? The Union Pacific in Wyoming? *Le Mistral* racketing through some Burgundian hamlet at sunset? The Pennsylvania parade at Princeton Junction? A Cotton Belt redball freight hustling up the Mississippi banks in Southeastern Missouri?

One of my superlatives deals with a series of American railroads that I seem persistently to lump together. All were in the Southeast; all preferred the U.S.R.A. patterns for their engines; all performed their railroading with a style that seems peculiarly Southern: they were, if you will, superlatively endowed with a regional flavor. These lines were Louisville and Nashville Railroad Co., the Nashville, Chattanooga and St. Louis Railway, Gulf Mobile and Ohio Railroad, and a group of three lines in the lower South that share facilities and are generally spoken of together: Atlanta and West Point Rail Road Co., the Western Railway of Alabama, and Georgia Railroad. I have listed six lines — which are now but five since L.&N. and N.C.&St.L. have merged. Let us treat them one by one.

LOUISVILLE AND NASHVILLE RAILROAD

I suppose that railroad buffs don't often think of the Louisville and Nashville for motive power elegance. The line's more passionate adherents would very much have it otherwise. And it was through some avid fans in Louisville that I first knew the line well. It was a winter's week end, bleak, windy and overcast, and they took me to see the dusky lines of panting and smoking road locomotives on the ready tracks at the

51

TERRELL DICKEY

THE MIGHTY M-1 — Engine 1965 was representative of L.&N.'s single venture into "Super Power." It could handle a remarkable variety of heavy-duty services: long coal "drags," fast merchandise freight, or long sections of *the Dixie Flyer.* This flattering photograph shows the great size of the sand dome (behind the smokestack) and the girth of the main rod, which leads from the crosshead just behind the cylinder to the third driving wheel. And 1965 has been given some of the decor usually associated with engines of an earlier vintage: stars on the wheel centers, polished bell and numeral

Tenth Street Station of L.&N. And then I saw the freights climbing Crescent Hill through the suburbs on the east side of Louisville. There were fine enough specimens of the U.S.R.A. light and heavy 2-8-2 types pulling, but they were grimy and soot stained. L.&N. let much of its power go to seed.

But then, on a warmer and brighter day, I saw some of the 400 series 4-8-2's — always to L.&N. men simply "the 400's." These were power for *The Pan American*, *The Dixie Flyer* and other L.&N. thoroughbred limiteds, and L.&N. consequently gave them a bit of the spit and polish that the Southern System and Chesapeake and Ohio more conspicuously brought into Louisville — all the whitened tires and running boards, the rubbed down jackets and, of course, the bright red L.&N. herald. You could always tell the L.&N. locomotives at a glance, with their big headlights and the rain cowl that surrounded their cab windows.

The line's single venture in locomotives of really high capacity resulted in something I think quite unusual. I speak of the M-1 2-8-4 Berkshire types, which were designed primarily for handling the long coal "drags" north from Corbin and other junction points in the coal fields of East Kentucky toward the Midwestern industrial centers. The M-1's seemed at once compact and massive — brutish but far from ugly. They were outfitted with "disk" driving wheels, cast in a craggy pattern that suggests some of the sculpture of this century. (Railway wheel and truck castings, in general, make me think of the Jacques Lipchitz of "Sailor with Guitar.") Brake cylinders were mounted on the exterior of the trailer truck and a vast cab that seemed vaguely "streamstyled" was mounted over that. The long tender, suspended over a pair of six-wheeled trucks, always seemed more like bridgework than railway rolling stock.

Regularly L.&N. relieved certain of the M-1 2-8-4's from the coal service and put them to handling heavy passenger trains through the hills of Eastern Kentucky. And such engines once pulled specials into Louisville for the Kentucky Derby. I am told the Berkshires managed splendidly in express service, keeping the schedules easily and making the soft starts that keep passenger traffic men smiling.

THE NASHVILLE, CHATTANOOGA AND ST. LOUIS RAILWAY

What the "Enn Cee and Saint Ell" did with locomotive streamlining was memorable. The line's problem was to do something modern with a new batch of engines to be built on the patterns used in the series of light 4-8-4's it had had built in 1930. Perhaps because this was wartime, N.C.&St.L. dispensed with some of the heavy frills and chroming of such other ventures into the streamlining of steam as Southern Railway 1380 and Chesapeake and Ohio 490. The engine draftsmen let the boiler top domes stay. A mildly pointed cone was attached to the front of the smokebox door. A yellow painted strip was attached below the running boards. The Vanderbilt-type tender was left unstreamlined but carried the yellow strip of the engine along its sides. That was all, but the engine seemed both in the railway tradition of the twenties and thirties and yet "contemporary" enough to complement the lightweight stainless steel coaches of the *Dixie Flagler*. Indeed, the N.C.&St.L. 570 series 4-8-4's seem to have constituted one of the most pleasing accomplishments in the modernizing of steam locomotives ever — quite in the class with the New Haven L-5 series Hudson types. The third set of 4-8-4's for the N.C.&St.L. — numbers 580-589 — had even less streamlining than the

WALTER H. THRALL, JR.

THE U.S.R.A. STYLE ON THE L.&N. — Neat and immaculate, L.&N. 407 is pictured as it stood on a ready track at Cincinnati, ready, perhaps, for a turn with *The Pan American*.

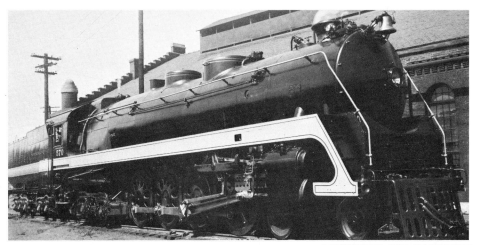

YELLOW JACKET — Here was a first-class accomplishment in the streamlining or stream-styling of the steam locomotive — a task rarely carried out with taste. The engine is number 570 of the N.C.&St.L., one of a series called "Yellow Jackets" because of the yellow strip that ran along the engine running board, cab and tender side. The locomotive seems almost British, its jacket is so clean of appliances and its livery is so muted. Compare it with the garish streamlining done for Chesapeake and Ohio 490, which is pictured in the Preface. But, despite its modern trim, there are definite traces of its U.S.R.A. ancestry.

YELLOW JACKET IN MICROCOSM — Two sets of rodding make almost corresponding sets of obtuse angles in this close-up view of part of the running gear of an N.C.&St.L. 4-8-4. This is a forceful example of the abundance of detail in shapes and proportions that the latter-day steam locomotive offered. The lower set of rods — the nearly horizontal "union rod" and the slanted "combining rod" — helped give motion to valves controlling steam going into the pistons. The upper set of silvered rods worked a mechanical lubricating device which relieved the engineer from alighting at each station stop and "oiling around" the running gear.

570 series. All of the 4-8-4's were dual service, which means they were equally competent to handle a 17-car limited or a long train of redball freight.

I am afraid that I found the other steam power of N.C.&St.L. rather homely. The U.S.R.A. Mountain types the line employed never seemed to benefit aesthetically from their spoked pilot wheels and capped stacks — European conventions applied to engines that simply didn't take well to them.

Fortunately, the engine that N.C.&St.L. has chosen to let survive is a specimen of the streamstyled 4-8-4 series. It stands behind a heavy (and necessary) fence in a park near the Parthenon in Nashville.

GULF MOBILE AND OHIO RAILROAD

It was almost as if Gulf Mobile and Ohio Railroad was a miniature of the Southern Railway System. What was it about the arched window and roof lines of the cab of a G.M.&O. Pacific type? And then the way the trailer truck was fabricated, the dome arrangement and the tender lines? Why, the engines were built nearly to the same patterns as those for the Southern System Ps-4 types. Indeed, they were identical except smaller. And when one looked at the G.M.&O. 2-8-2's the same was true; they were almost identical with the S.R. light U.S.R.A Mikes. Even the pre-1920 power for the line followed Southern's quite closely.

G.M.&O. followed, too, the fastidious maintenance of Southern. Roundhouse men liked to pick out the lines of the wheel tires and running boards in aluminum paint and burnish the running gear and bells.

There the comparison ends. For G.M.&O. had its own livery and its own herald. None of the Southern's fancy green for passenger power. The G.M.&O. stuck to proper black, and so in its passenger engines we could see how the Southern's green and gold power might have looked in black.

G.M.&O. has not usually been a prosperous line; in steam days its expresses were modest and its freights rather pokey. The wonder is that, even in the worst times of the depression of the thirties, the line kept its trains rolling with the style it did.* Perhaps the ante-bellum tradition of

*Gulf Mobile and Ohio was formed from a merger of the Gulf, Mobile and Northern and Mobile and Ohio railroads. Later G.M.&O. absorbed the Chicago and Alton.

THE SOUTHERN-LIKE LOCOMOTIVES OF THE MOBILE AND OHIO — Given different livery, the tidy 4-6-2 and 2-8-2 types pictured could easily pass for locomotives of the Southern Railway System. Both served the Mobile and Ohio, which later became part of the Gulf, Mobile and Northern.

the South demanded it. For the road steamed north from Mobile, up through Tuscaloosa and the Alabama of Carl Carmer's *Stars Fell on Alabama*. It had a leg into New Orleans, and the Northern terminus was the Mississippi River city of St. Louis. G.M.&O. knifed through Central Mississippi and the Faulkner country. Dinky Consolidation types chuffed over the branch to Starkville on the poorly ballasted, rocky line that passes through the Mississippi State College there. Gulf Mobile and Ohio was an indigent but immaculate noble.

Some of G.M.&O.'s territory prospers now, even though its once famous *Rebel,* one of the first diesel-powered streamliners, has gone. Somehow I feel the loss to diesels with especial keeness here. I'd give much to see one of the 260 series Pacifics "walking the dog" out of Pontotoc or Laurel.

THE WEST POINT ROUTE and GEORGIA RAILROAD

On the map, the two railroads of the West Point Route — The Atlanta and West Point Rail Road Co. and the Western Railway of Alabama — seem tiny. And Georgia Railroad even tinier. Yet in their modern history, quite as much as in their crucial years in the War Between the States, all three lines have conducted railroading in the big time style. And they have used modern, full-sized locomotives, although like a number of other railroads in the South and Southwest, they were loath to venture into "Super Power" steam.

Look over a collection of photographs of power for these lines. The 190 and 290 Pacific types indeed seem like steam power for some large system. Fair enough, for one of the great American passenger trains, *The Crescent*, has moved over the rails of The West Point Route. And the line has caught some of the heavy freight traffic in and out of Atlanta. Certainly West Point Route and its cousin, Georgia Railroad, have had much of the dash of the bigger lines they connect with, or rather "bridge" — Southern, Seaboard, Frisco, L.&N., A.C.L.

POWER FOR THE CRESCENT — Atlanta and West Point 290 — an enlarged version of the U.S.R.A. light 4-6-2 design — once handled the New York-New Orleans *Crescent* west from Atlanta.

MOTIVE POWER ELEGANCE

The real surprise and delight of each of these three lines was its fleet of ten wheeler types — lanky, with high wheels and the centered headlight and "bell up front" of the heavy, first-line road power. And sometimes for the ten wheelers there came important assignments — a second section of *The Crescent,* and their having to roll to the schedules the big Pacific types had to meet. Or double-heading with one of the U.S.R.A. Mikes to handle a fast and heavy freight on the line to Montgomery.

ENGLISH LIVERY AND ANTECEDENT — Close up of the lettering, numbering and line striping used by St. Louis-San Francisco locomotives during the later days of steam. The line striping with its peculiar fret work at the corners suggests the French Louis XVI and Directoire styles of decoration or, in the English speaking world, the Hepplewhite and Regency styles. Compare with the photograph below.

THE FRENCH INFLUENCE — This ebony and ormolu secretaire was typical of the French Louis XVI style, which has influenced so much decoration since — including fire engine and locomotive livery. Compare the panels of the secretaire with those of the locomotive and tender above.

CHAPTER 6

Steam's Directoire Period

Locomotives of The Frisco Lines

A CLEVER RAILROAD fan went amok one summer in Europe. In Kent he went to the Stewarts Lane engine sheds of the London-Dover line. It was late at night, and it took him a few minutes to attach the chime whistle of an American locomotive to the boiler of *Harrow*, an express engine. The next day *Harrow* coupled up to a boat train for Dover, but the whistle was so unexpected that the tower man switched this train onto the wrong track and it ended up at Bury St. Edmunds.

In Rome, our zealot donned a black uniform and went to the railroad station and to the platforms where the electric trains into the Campagna leave. He yelled "All aboard!" in a hoarse voice, first by the 5:12 p.m. for Frascati and then by the 5:15 p.m. for Velletri. It so confused all the Frascati commuters that they got the 5:15 for Velletri by mistake. And the Velletri commuters all got the 5:12 for Frascati by mistake.

It was at the Gare de Perrache in Lyon that this enthusiast next struck. He simply couldn't resist the tenders of the locomotives at the nearby engine terminal. Early one morning he painted "Baltimore and Ohio" in neat, serifed letters on the tender of one engine. "Lackawanna" went onto another French tender. And, in large yellow sans-serif letters, "Union Pacific" on a third. The French thought it was the work of Algerians, some American tourists and servicemen were at first astonished and then amused, and the local engine dispatcher got all mixed up. An engine that was to be coaled and watered went out on the *Mistral* instead and ran out of fuel in the tunnel at Vienne, and an engine that was to go out on the *Mistral* went back a second time to the coal dock and was buried under a superfluous avalanche of that fuel.

61

Our fan turned his attention to Burgundy next. But there his enthusiasm waned and his heart broke.

He rode the steam cars to Nevers. Being cultivated and curious both, he wanted to see the imposing but badly ruined Gothic cathedral. He did that. And then he saw the fine, eighteenth-century *hôtel* that houses the museum, and finally the medieval fortifications. Now he turned his attention to the train station. It was memorable: long lines of live steam at the terminal beyond the passenger train shed — Pacifics, Mountain types and 2-8-2's. Some moving up the ready tracks, some working through the sander, the coal dock and the standpipe, some approaching the train shed. Off to the west, the staccato puffs of a hard-working freight engine rose and fell in volume against factories and a cut in the right-of-way.

It seemed too much, for Nevers not only taunted him with the French medieval heritage but also the heritage of American steam railroading. As for the engines, it was all just like Lindenwood . . .

But he knew there was nothing back at Lindenwood — or nothing with steam up anyway — and there hadn't been for years. Three grimy 4-8-4's rusted away near the turntable. Inside the roundhouse a 4-8-2 waited for transportation to some damn-fool city park.

It must be said that our man was a shameless nostalgic — the incurable provinicial who, on the Boulevard Haussmann in April, dreams of the daffodils at Toddsbury and Brandon. But then he was a Frisco fan, and, in the days of steam on the Frisco, there was just nothing else in the world quite comparable.

If, as David Morgan says, the Southern Railway was our "most persuasively beautiful carrier" in steam, then the St. Louis-San Francisco Railway was surely our *second* most persuasively beautiful carrier. The Frisco, it seemed, could do no wrong. It rebuilt old and small locomotives of awkward lines into larger and more powerful machines of unassailable good looks. Its heavy, World War II, 4500 series of 4-8-4 types were classical, taking the best of the U.S.R.A. and "Super Power" both — fully equal in grace to the New York Central Hudsons and the Nickle Plate 2-8-4's. And then there were the 1500's.

It wasn't that the 1500 series of 4-8-2's were really painted blue with gold trim, although we remember them that way. I am indebted to

E. G. Baker, who reminds me that the 1500's had jackets of Russian iron of a bluish hue and *seemed* to be painted blue. But the other things we remember about the 1500's were quite true: the really almost effeminate decor — the striped panels on tender sides and cab, with a sort of Greek fret at the corners that seemed Louis XVI, Directoire or Regency in spirit if not in literal detail. The incredible care with which metal work was polished, the jaunty numerals on the tender sides, and the red trim of the medallion-like numeral plate.

Perhaps no other locomtives in America — even the Southern Railway Ps-4's and the R.F.&P. 4-8-4's — were given more meticulous styling and grooming. And yet, with all these remarkable points, it took some publicity for the world to know of the Frisco 1500's. These engines were virtually "undiscovered" until Lucius Beebe began featuring them in his earlier books, *High Iron* and *Trains in Transition*. And until Mr. Baker and the team of Nansen and Barham began photographing them before and during World War II. Now they are among the best-remembered locomotives of the latter days of steam in America. Actually, they were rather awkward when viewed simply as locomotives. The tenders seemed too small to carry the over-large trucks. The cab was tall and gawky and the stack overbearing. But given the livery Frisco used for its passenger power, the 1500's were splendid to look at.

As was so with the Southern, Frisco's passenger style was more visual than actual. In Donald M. Steffee's speed surveys of the thirties and early forties—the years when the 1500's were hauling premium trains—the Frisco passenger trains were never in the columns listing runs at 60 miles an hour or more. The relatively low, 70-inch driving wheels of the 1500's were fine for getting the *Will Rogers* over heavy grades in the Ozarks. But they weren't much for speed.

Frisco's "varnish" still doesn't make the speed columns. Actually, the line was and still is fast (although not fast*est*) for freight. It *means* that slogan, "Frisco Faster Freight." One of the news events of the later steam era was the headline that told of Frisco merchandise freight handled by passenger Pacific types, and moving on virtually passenger-train schedules. Frisco's fast movements of California perishables over routes

THE 1500-SERIES: The Directoire Style on the Frisco Lines — Passenger power on St. Louis-San Francisco Railway could readily be identified by the distinctively striped panels on the tender and cab, which carried a fretted motif at the corners. Boiler jackets on these locomotives were a dark-blue Russian iron. The sans-serif lettering on the cab was gilded and so were the Bank-modernish numerals on the tender. The cab window, sash and number plate were red and the plate edged with white. The bell and running gear were immaculately shined. Such engines handled both the *Texas Special* and the *Will Rogers*.

PRESTON GEORGE

BLACK AND GOLD — A beautifully groomed St. Louis-San Francisco 1500 series 4-8-2 at speed with a local passenger train in Oklahoma in 1946.

operated jointly with the Texas and Pacific and Southern Pacific systems have been famous — notably the "Colton Block" and the "Imperial Valley."

Is it ever said enough? One of the joys of steam locomotive watching in America was the great variety in the machines themselves. The standardization of the locomotives of the U.S.R.A. was really extraordinary in our steam history. For the rule throughout has been custom building—new patterns and jigs for virtually each class of motive power. Certainly, Frisco's engines were distinctive—and readily recognized without paint or livery. The cab, domes and stack were all taller than those for most other locomotives — features the generous clearances of the line allowed for. The tenders, for the most part, carried oil and, oddly, seemed even when new to have been built for coal hauling (they had the "profile" of coal hauling tenders), and then converted to oil as an afterthought.

But within its standardization, what a variety of steam power the St. Louis-San Francisco had to roll over its "X" shaped system. There were 2-10-2's to handle coal drags from Southeastern Missouri and the connections there with the Illinois coal fields. Then the World War II 4-8-4's for manifest freight north from Pensacola and Birmingham, and heavy sections of the *Meteor* southwest of St. Louis into the cities of Oklahoma and Texas. The catalog is impressive. The homemade heavy 4-8-2's the line rebuilt from 2-10-2's, the low drivered Hudson types rebuilt from the larger 4-6-2's; 4-6-0's, 2-6-0's, 2-8-0's, 0-6-0's — Frisco had them all.

Certainly one remembers with particular vividness the line's 4200 series of Mikes, which were among the heaviest engines of the 2-8-2 wheel arrangement ever built. Stocky, chunky, with ample tenders, they seemed the quintessence of railway force and thrust. And yet they were far from ugly.

We have a remarkable record of all this steam power in the photographs of Robert J. Foster, who covered the Frisco steam roster exhaustively and with great precision.* Mr. Foster liked to find locomotives freshly shopped and liked to view them from the right side and with the drivers at midstroke in the "down" position.

Our train buff on the loose in Europe had known most of this steam power at the Lindenwood, Missouri, roundhouse. Little wonder (our story is not entirely fictional) that France gave him something of a heartbreak.

Sigmund Freud, who analyzed many other things in his lifetime, once tried an analysis of the train fascination. In *Contributions to the Theory of Sex*, Freud wrote: "Shaking sensations experienced in wagons and railroad trains exert such a fascinating influence on older children that all boys, at least at one time in their lives, wish to become conductors and drivers [engineers]. They are wont to ascribe to railroad activities an extraordinary and mysterious interest, and during the age of phantastic activity (shortly before puberty) they utilize these as a nucleus for exquisite sexual symbolisms. The desire to connect railroad traveling with sexuality apparently originates from the pleasurable character of the sensation of motion."

*Mr. Foster's valuable record of steam power has included many other Midwestern, Western and Southern lines.

ENGINE AND BED — (above) This immaculate, seemingly austere locomotive was the most powerful steam engine that ever served St. Louis-San Francisco Railway — a high-capacity machine that could keep up speeds of 55 miles-per-hour or more with trains of more than 100 freight cars. (below) The "Commonwealth" bed casting that served as the foundation for this locomotive — typical of the handsome castings that American suppliers have contributed and are still contributing to railways all over the world.   The series of holes at the center carried driving boxes which housed the diving wheel axles, and the front section of the boiler, or smokebox, was attached at the "saddle" between the cylinders. This casting replaced what in earlier locomotives was an intricately-fabricated structure.

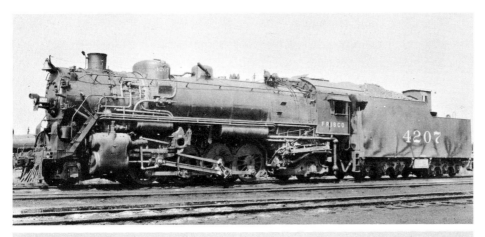

(ALL VIEWS, ROBERT J. FOSTER)

THE MODERN STEAM LOCOMOTIVE ON THE FRISCO — (above) the 4200-series heavy 2-8-2. (center) 4400-series 4-8-2 with "Scullins" driving wheels, rebuilt from a 2-10-2 type. (below) Modernized Pacific type in passenger livery.

Now this is all, of course, to be viewed in the context of Freud's mission and accomplishments. But surely he has loaded the case here a bit. And surely Freud never knew the black and gold 1500's of the Frisco lines the way *we* did. Not with *that* critical method.

CHAPTER 7

The Dash Of The
Missouri - Kansas - Texas Line

U P AHEAD a compact 2-8-2 rigged out with smoke deflectors
steamed gracefully through the reverse curves of a hilly railroad.
I stood in the aisle at the window in the last of a long string of olive
green coaches and watched the drivers work as the engine covered a
turn into a tunnel. Darkness — and we coughed from the grimy oil
smoke. Then light and relief — our train rolled out onto a tall stone
bridge, a nimble worm on a toy aqueduct. It rained softly in this green,
if rocky land, and I could easily hear the steady rattle of the engine exhausts. We slowed, stopped at some gay junction town amid raucous
greetings, while luggage was handed down to the station platform
through open car windows. Then sharp exhausts rapped out ahead as
the Mike strained and shuddered to get the train rolling again. The
landscape flattened, the train sped onto straight trackage, and l could
no longer see the engine . . .

This happened in 1961, but, alas, not in America. Probably I revealed this to you when I said that I stood in the aisle at the window of
my coach. The scene was west of Cannes on the Paris-Riviera line of
the French National Railways; the engine was, of course, one of the
hundreds of fine American-styled and American-built Mikes still operating daily in France.

I was nostalgic and a little melancholy during that summer afternoon in Provence. For my mind went back to what had once been
the Missouri-Kansas-Texas Railroad in steam — that gallant, energetic,
single-tracked line hustling its neat limiteds and redball freights through
the Ozarks and across the Oklahoma prairies. I thought of the gleaming Mikes and Pacifics carrying the dazzling scarlet "Katy" herald

EDWARDIAN MODES OF ENGINE LIVERY IN GREAT BRITAIN AND AMERICA — (above) Midland Railway 1000, a 4-4-0 of the year 1901, illustrates perfectly the British penchant for fastidious engine livery. The only decorations are numerals on the tender, striped panels on engine and tender and thin white bands on the wheel tires. The modest Midland herald is within the panel beneath the cab window. The engine jacket and tender were painted Burgundy wine red. (below) Pictured in 1939, Missouri-Kansas-Texas 312, an engine of about 1890, shows an American adaptation of the English Edwardian livery. Here are similar numerals on the tender, modest initials for the railroad on the cab and a silvering of running boards and tires. In addition, the smokebox has been painted with a special graphite-gray paint, and the cab windows scarlet. American livery had been gaudy in the eighteen seventies and eighties but assumed the austere British modes about 1895, and for the most part kept them until the end of steam.

on their tender sides. Lucius Beebe, I believe, remembers the steam days of the Katy with a particular fondness. And I with him.

I suppose the Katy was everything one now recalls in using the term "Standard Railroading." Even into the nineteen fifties, it pulled its trains behind what were the usual road engines of the teens and the early twenties — 4-6-2's and 2-8-2's of modest proportions, and bereft of the more bizarre and experimental efficiency appliances that other steam roads tried. Its expresses were made up of "standard" olive green steel coaches and Pullmans of circa 1915. And, the M-K-T rolled them with the pride and dash of the Pennsylvania or the Southern Pacific. Mr. Beebe and I have not been alone in our admiration for this line. For Katy has been one of those special darlings among American railfans—persistently beloved, like the Denver and Rio Grande Western narrow gauge, the Rutland, or the C.N.O.&T.P. Division of the Southern Railway System.

Certainly the Katy had style — perhaps as much as anything in the branch line service. Its trim Moguls, 4-4-0's and 4-6-0's — steaming across the Oklahoma plains to such places as Altus, Elk City, Enid—rated all the maintenance and care given to the first-line, mainline road power. Preston George has photographed them appealingly, with their two-or-three-car trains of big old wooden coaches, as they streaked across the Southwestern badlands. George's photographs of the Katy capture a mode of railroading that could easily be in South Africa or the remoter districts of Mexico. So, too, this perfection with the Katy switchers; these were also scrupulously maintained and given the scarlet herald on their tender sides.

But we remember the M-K-T best for the steam power on its mainline operations — the freight engines as much as the passenger. Indeed, Katy thought so much of its fast freight service that even back in the thirties, when passenger trains were still considered the prestige service of the railroad industry, the road advertised its freight schedules at the head of its listing in the railway *Official Guide*.

Perhaps the Katy's last series of 4-6-2 types were aesthetically the perfect locomotives of that wheel arrangement in America. These engines were smaller by a good deal than the 4-6-2 giants of the C.&O. F-19 series or the 600 series of the Chicago, Minneapolis, St. Paul and

Omaha. But their lines — including the short cab, the tidy domes, the neat smokebox front — were flawless. Only the Southern Railway Ps-4's or the Missouri Pacific P-73's were their peers in perfection of design. This can't be said for the Katy 2-8-2's, which, it seemed to me, always suffered somewhat in having large and awkward cabs and rather chopped-down tenders.

Why were there never any really big steam locomotives for the M-K-T? The line had full-length trains and ambitious schedules, and there were certainly respectable enough grades. Somehow, like the Southern Railway System and the lines of the West Point Route, the Katy never cared to venture into what the advertisements of Lima Locomotive Works called "Super Power." It ran its steam nobly, without the benefit of modern, high-capacity locomotives with large fireboxes riding over four-wheeled trucks — the 4-8-4, 2-8-4 or 4-6-6-4 types that almost every other comparable road in America had tried at least once before the diesel came.

Strange that the demise of passenger service in America seems to have followed so surely the demise of the steam locomotive. Katy's seems a classic example of the progressive curtailment of passenger service in this country since 1945. I suppose we can call 1939 the last full year for Standard Railroading, for after that the diesel locomotive and the stainless steel passenger car began remaking the style of American railroading. In that prewar year, the Katy ran three trains daily each way between Kansas City and Texas and between St. Louis and Texas

E. G. BAKER

KATY'S BEST — Pacific type 379 was first-line passenger power for the Missouri-Kansas-Texas Railroad. The locomotive featured such typical M-K-T decoration as the scarlet herald on the tender, large numerals under the cab window, aluminum paint on wheel tires and running boards.

(the St. Louis and Kansas City trains joined up in northern Oklahoma for the run southward to Texas). And there were passenger trains on more than a dozen branch lines.

In the last issue of the *Official Guide* available (November 1961), there were but four Katy passenger train schedules listed — those of the *Texas Special* and a local each way from Kansas City to San Antonio.

One other thing the Katy brings to mind: There developed some years back a genre of thriller fiction that dealt with railroads. It was chiefly found in *Railroad Magazine* and *The Saturday Evening Post;* the best known authors were E. S. Dellinger, Harry Bedwell and Gilbert A. Lathrop. One remembers fondly their "Oil Belt and Western" and "Ozark Lines" railroads, the division point at "Oldberg" and the mountain telegraph station at "Canyon." We think nostalgically of "Poor Eddie Sand," one of Bedwell's most notable characters, a railway telegraph operator. "So competent, so well disposed, and yet constantly either in trouble or restless and moving about from place to place." Above all, the stories of the writers of this school ran thoroughly true to the flavor of American railroading in this century. They were perfectly "researched," as the book jacket blurbs put it.

Well, we have had good railroad fiction. But never the authentic *movie* of railroading as Americans practiced it in the first half of this century. I am not speaking of the corny, Wild West railroad movie—the progress of a dinky, second-hand, branch-line "teakettle" with modern couplings, given a period paint job and asked to portray the role of the locomotive on a pioneer transcontinental line. Nor of the gunman's

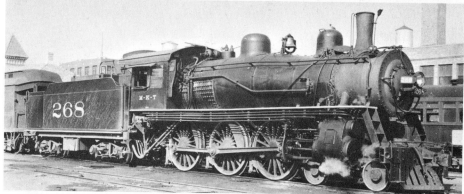

SMALLER STEAM ON M-K-T (above) U.S.R.A.-type switcher with Katy herald on the tender. (below) Ten wheeler with numerals on the tender.

ride on a rickety, alleged Wells Fargo express car that rolls on modern cast steel trucks. This is the hyper-quaint image of nineteenth-century railroading that makes the "Tweetsie" exhibition narrow gauge railroad in North Carolina feel obliged to equip its 2-8-2 type from Alaska with a faked diamond stack which it never used in the service for which it was built.

What I want to see is the drama of running a smart mainline steam railroad with smart equipment, smart locomotives and tight, demanding schedules, the sort of drama that only last year James McCague created in his novel *Fiddle Hill*. Whatever be the fictional overlay, a wonderful movie could be made in just the portrayal of railroading techniques. I mean the firing and running of a modern steam locomotive, the skills of signaling and dispatching, of switching and train makeup. Certainly

(center) AUTHOR; (second from bottom) LOUISVILLE AND NASHVILLE

PACIFIC TYPES ON THE U.S.R.A. PATTERN — (from top) Missouri-Kansas-Texas — 400-series when built; Missouri-Kansas-Texas — 400-series in the nineteen thirties with tender on Dalman-type trucks; Southern Railway — Ps-4 series for the Eastern Lines (1928) with straight running boards, single-guide crossheads and built-up coal bunker; Louisville and Nashville — K-5 series with U.S.R.A. cab and enlarged tender; Atlanta and West Point — after the Heavy U.S.R.A. design with "Delta" trailing truck under the cab and tender on "Commonwealth" swing-motion trucks.

the movie should show the grace of the twentieth-century locomotive in action: the almost living stride that so resembles the motion of a horse. Ingmar Bergman has shown the way in the excellent, if brief, train sequence in the movie "Dreams."

If the movies ever do a study of Standard Railroading, I nominate the M-K-T for the setting. The properties man may have to mock up a Katy 4-6-2 to handle the *Katy Flyer*. And perhaps repaint a Fort Worth and Denver City 2-8-2 to speed into the camera with a fictional St. Louis-Dallas freight. Let them also bring back the double-headed 4-4-0's that served the branch lines.

Throw in a footloose telegraph "op" with patent leather hair and green eyeshade, a lovely stationmaster's daughter who can take the heart of even the most hardened "boomer" brakeman, a trembling student fireman and, by all means, a stern, fiery division superintendent who intimidates directors and night yardmasters alike. Give us a runaway cut of freight cars, and an heroic switch crew that rounds them up just in time to prevent their smashing into the *Flyer*. But let us have that movie of big-time steam railroading as it was in the thirties. And be sure that Katy is the star.

Bibliography

THE SELECTIONS offered here are not meant to be exhaustive; they represent materials that have been made available to the author.

MACHINE DESIGN AND AMERICAN TASTE: Sigfried Giedion's books, *Space, Time and Architecture*, third edition, revised (Boston, 1954) and *Mechanization Takes Command* (New York, 1948), can be regarded as seminal — the considered views of a serious and highly regarded critic of architecture, city planning and design. There are valuable insights in James Marston Fitch's *Architecture and the Aesthetics of Plenty* (New York, 1961), especially in the chapter "The Aesthetics of Plenty," pp. 268-284. Russell Lynes's *The Tastemakers* (New York, 1954) is a brilliantly written popular history of taste in America — the off-the-cuff commentary of a literate and judicious observer. In *Virginia: a new look at the Old Dominion* (New York, 1959), especially the chapter entitled "Restoration Blues" (pp. 243-254), Marshall W. Fishwick offers fascinating reasons as to why the Queen Anne taste has continued in the whole South and particularly in Virginia.

LOCOMOTIVE DESIGN IN AMERICA: David P. Morgan's article "What is a Good Looking Locomotive?" from *Railroad Magazine*, Vol. 45, No. 2 (March 1948), pp. 46-58, is an early study and still perhaps the most important single writing on the aesthetic aspects of this subject. The author's "The Architecture of the Locomotive," *Trains*, Vol. 16, No. 6 (April, 1956), pp. 26-30, offers a number of conclusions that have been the basis for this book. The books of Lucius Beebe (mentioned below) often give excellent observations.

THE STEAM LOCOMOTIVE IN AMERICA, 1918-1945, IN GENERAL: Mr. Beebe's series of books have come to be regarded as standard in this field, and they offer an unparalleled photographic record of American steam power in this century — most of it at speed and with trains. The Beebe books have given generous coverage to the railroads especially treated in this book. Mr. Beebe's facts are occasionally inaccurate, but his critical observations are invariably sound. The relevant titles are: *High Iron* (New York, 1938), *Highliners* (New York, 1940), *Trains in Transition* (New York, 1941), *Highball* (New York, 1945), and the culminating book in the series, *The Age of Steam* (New York, 1958). *The Last of Steam* by Joe G. Collins (Berkeley, California, 1960) offers an abundance of action photographs of steam, mostly in the 1945-1955 period. *Steam, Steel & Limiteds* by William W. Kratville (Omaha), which was to be ready in early 1962, should offer much material, not only on the locomotives of this period but also passenger equipment. The author's "Standard Railroading," from *Trains*, Vol. 14, No. 11 (September, 1954), pp. 22-26, is in part concerned with the locomotive, being a discussion of the flavor of American railroading in the twenties and thirties.

Steam's Finest Hour (Milwaukee, 1959), edited by Mr. Morgan, offers a lavish selection of large-sized photographs of American steam locomotives during the period concerned in this book, and benefits from the editor's literate and highly informed commentary and intelligent organization of his materials. Another storehouse of large-sized locomotive pictures (including many giving details and appliances) is *Model Railroader Cyclopedia, Vol. 1,* (Milwaukee, 1961), edited by Lynn H. Westcott. This shows many locomotive and tender plans unavailable in print elsewhere. *American Locomotives, 1900-1950* (New York, 1950), edited by Edwin P. Alexander, suffers from scant data and often poor photography, but is useful in that it shows the year-by-year development of the American steam locomotive.

The *Locomotive Cyclopedia* series of Simmons-Boardman Publishing Corp. are really indispensable for any survey of this kind; these include specifications for a wide variety of American and American-export engines and much detail on locomotive parts and appliances. Perhaps the 1941 issue would be most valuable for further study of the engines treated in this book. Walter A. Lucas's 100-*Years of Steam Locomotives* (New York, 1957) is a digest of the *Locomotive Cyclopedia* series. The best popular exposition of the mechanics of steam locomotion known to the author is Alfred W. Bruce's *The Steam Locomotive in America* (New York, 1950), and the chapter "Meet the Modern Iron Horse," pp.

119-148, in *Steel Trails* by Martin D. Stevers (New York, 1933) is useful. A somewhat more technical discussion of the mechanics of the steam engine is offered in the chapter "The Reciprocating Steam Locomotive" pp. 239-318, by C. R. H. Simpson from *The Concise Encyclopedia of World Railways,* edited by E. Ransome Wallis (New York, 1959). Mr. Simpson is primarily concerned with British practice but by no means ignores American developments. There is much engineering data in Ralph P. Johnson's *The Steam Locomotive: Its Theory, Operation and Economics, Including Comparisons with Diesel Electric Locomotives* (New York, 1942).

Mr. Morgan's "Annual Motive Power Survey," which is an episodic feature of *Trains,* has given in its entirety a definitive running commentary on the end of steam in America and the beginnings of successive forms of locomotion. It has been published since 1949. There is an informative, concise account of the development of the high-capacity steam locomotive in the nineteen twenties on pages 18-21 of "Sixty Years of Lima Locomotives" by Earle Davis, from *Railroad Magazine,* Vol. 27, No. 1 (December, 1939).

LOCOMOTIVES OF THE UNITED STATES RAILWAY ADMINISTRATION: Two articles have given this movement abundant coverage: William D. Edson's "The U.S.R.A. Locomotives," which appeared in *The Railway and Locomotive Historical Society Bulletin,* No. 93 (October, 1955), pp. 73-93; and "The Very First U.S.R.A. Engine" by Frederick Westing, from *Trains,* Vol. 21, No. 2 (December, 1960), pp. 47-51.

RAILWAY FICTION: Historians seeking the atmosphere of railroading in the 1917-1945 period will have to look up the railroad fiction concerned with the era, which is low in literary value but high in documentary accuracy. James McCague's novel *Fiddle Hill* (New York, 1960) gives an unassailably accurate portrayal of mountain railroading toward the last days of steam. *Railroad Magazine* has carried much of the most pertinent fiction. The following is a sampler: E. S. Dellinger, "The Ballast Scorcher," from Vol. 27, No. 2 (January, 1940), pp.

76-99; Ed Samples, "Whitecliff Pass," from Vol. 25, No. 4 (March, 1939), pp. 78-104, and "Railroad Avenue," from Vol. 27, No. 5 (April, 1940), pp. 6-31; John Johns, "Orders at Canyon," from Vol. 28, No. 2 (July, 1940), pp. 104-115, and "Four Track Stuff," from Vol. 29, No. 6 (May, 1941), pp. 26-41; Gilbert A. Lathrop, "Throttle Artist," from Vol. 34, No. 4 (September, 1943), pp. 44-63. Harry Bedwell, "The Yardmaster's Story," from Vol. 26, No. 3 (August, 1939), pp. 82-107. Mr. Bedwell's "Eddie Sand" stories were a feature of *Railroad Magazine* during the nineteen thirties. Among Mr. Bedwell's stories for *The Saturday Evening Post* were "Snow on the High Iron," from Vol. 213, No. 24 (December 14, 1940), pp. 18-19 and 39-44; and "Lantern in His Hand," from Vol. 215, No. 30 (January 23, 1943), pp. 22-23 and 66-68.

THE RAILROADS TREATED IN THIS BOOK: The series of locomotive rosters published over the years in *Railroad Magazine* are of first importance in any study of the engines of a particular American railroad, unless a detailed, book-length monograph has been prepared. The *Railroad Magazine* rosters were usually checked or compiled by the motive power departments of the lines concerned, and they have usually been complete and accurate. Extended studies of the steam motive power of several of the railroads treated in this book are curiously lacking.

THE SOUTHERN RAILWAY SYSTEM: The author's "Ps-4," from *Trains*, Vol. 10, No. 12 (October, 1950), pp. 20-26, gives detailed coverage of the important Southern Railway Ps-4 class of 4-6-2 locomotives. *Railroad Magazine* rosters: June and July, 1938, and March and April, 1950, issues.

RICHMOND, FREDERICKSBURG AND POTOMAC RAILROAD: Two monographs by John B. Mordecai, *A Brief History of the Richmond, Fredericksburg and Potomac Railroad* (Richmond, 1941) and *Richmond, Fredericksburg and Potomac Railroad in the Second World War* (Richmond, 1948), offer historical material on the R.F.&P. and give a few factual locomotive details. Paul T. Warner's "Pacific Type Locomotives on The Richmond, Fredericksburg and Potomac Railroad," from the January, 1926, issue of *Baldwin Locomotives*, pp. 64-70, treats this phase of the line's locomotive development exhaustively. "Capitol Cities Route," from *Trains*, Vol. 2, No. 1 (November, 1941), pp. 32-37, by Wiley M. Bryan, gives a railroad fireman's observations on the locomotives of this line. A comparative survey of the 4-8-4 types of the line is offered in the short feature "Statesmen," from *Railroad Magazine*, Vol. 36, No. 6 (November, 1945), pp. 50-51. *Railroad Magazine* roster: November, 1932, issue.

THE CHESAPEAKE AND OHIO RAILROAD: Charles W. Turner's *Chessie's Road* (Richmond, 1956) is mostly history and offers only a few facts on the C.&O. locomotives. *Railroad Magazine* rosters: October, 1944, and May, 1948, issues.

SEABOARD AIR LINE RAILWAY: *Railroad Magazine* roster: September, 1948 issue.

ATLANTIC COAST LINE RAILROAD: Mr. Warner's "Locomotive Development on the Atlantic Coast Line Railroad" takes this subject through most of the line's steam locomotive history, neglecting only the 1800-series 4-8-4's of 1938 and wartime or merger acquisitions; *Baldwin Locomotives*, January, 1926, issue, pp. 3-26. *Railroad Magazine* roster: December, 1938, issue.

LOUISVILLE AND NASHVILLE RAILROAD: L.&N. benefits from both a general history — *Louisville and Nashville Railroad 1850-1959* by Kincaid Herr (Louisville, 1959)—and a motive power survey — *Louisville and Nashville Steam Locomotives* by Richard E. Prince (Green River, Wyoming, 1959). Both give extensive coverage, and Mr. Prince's book is exhaustive as to detail, modifications, dates. *Railroad Magazine* roster: January, 1936, issue.

NASHVILLE, CHATTANOOGA AND ST. LOUIS RAILWAY: Mr. Warner's "The Locomotives of the Nashville, Chattanooga and St. Louis Railway" gives excellent coverage of developments up through 1927. *Baldwin Locomotives*, July, 1927. "State-Owned Railroad," by Herbert G. Monroe in Vol. 29, No. 1 (December, 1945) of *Railroad Magazine*, pp. 8-44, is a feature-type survey of the N.C.&St.L. *Railroad Magazine* roster: October, 1939, issue.

THE WEST POINT ROUTE AND GEORGIA RAILROAD:
Mr. Prince's *Steam Locomotives and History — Georgia Railroad and West Point Route* (Green River, Wyoming) was to be published in early 1962. It should be factual and definitive. *Railroad Magazine* roster: December, 1939, issue.

GULF, MOBILE AND OHIO RAILROAD: *Railroad Magazine* rosters: Gulf, Mobile and Northern, May, 1934, issue; Mobile and Ohio, September, 1934, issue.

ST. LOUIS-SAN FRANCISCO RAILROAD: A monograph on the steam power of the St.L.-S.F. is badly needed. *Railroad Magazine* roster: July, 1948, issue.

MISSOURI-KANSAS-TEXAS RAILROAD: *Railroad Magazine* roster: October, 1934, issue.

ENGLISH AND CONTINENTAL RAILWAYS: The amount of literature on the railways of Great Britain is simply staggering, but several book titles seem to stand out as especially relevant to this book. *Locomotives in Retirement* by E. W. Fenton (London, 1958) offers large full-page, full-color plates of ten locomotives of the British late Victorian and Edwardian eras, showing all the details of their highly decorative livery. *British Steam Horses* by George Dow (London, 1950) is a popular discussion of latter-day British steam power, treating both the standardized designs for the nationalized railways and the first-line locomotives of the four great English systems before nationalization. There is also some exposition of locomotive practices. Several books of O. S. Nock seem highly pertinent and valuable—notably *British Railways in Action* (London, 1956), *The Locomotives of Sir Nigel Gresley* (London, 1945), *Locomotives of the North Eastern Railway* (London), and *Steam Locomotive* (London). Cecil J. Allen's *Locomotive Practice and Performance in the Twentieth Century* (London), is the work of a leading authority on railway speed and schedules.

BIBLIOGRAPHY

The author has little knowledge of the literature of the French railways, but one volume has much to commend it. The is *Le Matérial Moteur S.N.C.F.* by Jacques Defrance (Paris, 1960), which is an illustrated roster of all the steam, electric and diesel locomotives of the S.N.C.F. (The French National Railways).

A Note

About Locomotive Wheel Arrangememts and Symbols and the Locomotive Builders

AMERICAN steam locomotives have traditionally been identified by the Whyte System, *viz*: If the wheel arrangement of an engine is o OOOOO o, meaning two wheels beneath the cylinders, 10 driving wheels and two wheels beneath the firebox, it is, according to the Whyte system, a 2-10-2. It is also, like engines of other wheel arrangements, known universally by some identifying name — in this case "Santa Fe" because engines of such wheel arrangement were first used on the Atchison, Topeka and Santa Fe Railroad.

Locomotives most often described in this book are:

OOO	0-6-0	Six Wheeled Switcher
OOOO	0-8-0	Eight Wheeled Switcher
o OOOO	2-8-0	Consolidation Type
o OOOO o	2-8-2	Mikado Type or Mike
o OOOO oo	2-8-4	Berkshire Type
oo OOO	4-6-0	Ten Wheeler
oo OOO o	4-6-2	Pacific Type
oo OOO oo	4-6-4	Hudson Type
oo OOOO o	4-8-2	Mountain Type
oo OOOO oo	4-8-4	Northern Type

Most railroads give their engines symbols, according to wheel arrangement. "J-2" would indicate most likely the second design of whatever the "J" wheel arrangement happens to be. "J-2a" would be a modification of the J-2 class.

The term "U.S.R.A." refers always to the United States Railway Administration (see preface), under whose sponsorship came the basic patterns for many engines treated in this book.

The principal American builders of steam locomotives during the period this book spans were The Baldwin Locomotive Works (known as "BLW" or simply "Baldwin"), American Locomotive Company ("American" or "Alco"), and The Lima Locomotive Works, Inc. ("Lima"). Later Lima became Lima-Hamilton and still later, in the merger with Baldwin, Baldwin-Lima-Hamilton Corp.

Acknowledgments

I SHOULD like to acknowledge my indebtedness to the following for assistance with photographs and research: Stuart Shumate, president of the Richmond, Fredericksburg and Potomac Railroad; J. Dan House of General Steel Industries, Inc.; Buckeye Steel Castings Co., Inc., and August A. Thieme, Jr. Charles B. Castner, Jr., now of the advertising and publications department of Louisville and Nashville Railroad, Professor Charles W. Turner and Henry Hope Reed, Jr., were kind enough to read parts of the manuscript in progress and offer suggestions. I have drawn heavily on Mr. Castner's knowledge of locomotives and train operations on the L.&N. and the former Nashville, Chattanooga and St. Louis Railway. Especial mention is due Eliza Little for editorial assistance of high value and competence, E. G. Baker for his thorough notes on the locomotives of the St. Louis-San Francisco Railroad, and David P. Morgan, editor of *Trains*, whose correspondence and published writings over the years have been the inspiration for this book. It is owing to Lee H. Murch of the Barre Gazette, who encouraged the book from the very start, that *The Georgian Locomotive* progressed from a conception to an accomplished fact.

The quotation from Sigmund Freud on page 67 is from *The Basic Writings of Sigmund Freud*, trans. and ed. by Dr. A. A. Brill, Copyright 1938 by Random House, Inc. Reprinted by permission of the Brill Trust. The quotation from Aldous Huxley on page 49 is from *Theme and Variations*, published by Harper & Brothers. Certain material in the Preface appeared originally in *Trains Magazine*.